The Complete Book Of
Foosball

The Complete Book Of
Foosball

Johnny Lott
with Kathy Brainard

Contemporary Books, Inc.
Chicago

Library of Congress Cataloging in Publication Data

Lott, Johnny.
  The complete book of foosball.

  Includes index.
  1. Foosball (Game)   I. Brainard, Kathy, joint author.   II. Title.
  GV1469.4.L67   794   80-65934
  ISBN 978-0-9814711-0-5

Copyright © 1980 by Johnny Rafols (writing as Johnny Lott) and Kathy Brainard
All rights reserved
Published by Contemporary Books, Inc.
180 North Michigan Avenue, Chicago, Illinois 60601
Manufactured in the United States of America
Library of Congress Catalog Card Number: 80-65934
International Standard Book Number: 0-8092-5999-0 (cloth)
                                     0-8092-5998-2 (paper)

Published simultaneously in Canada by
Beaverbooks
953 Dillingham Road
Pickering, Ontario L1W 1Z7
Canada

Contents

    Introduction   ix
1. History of Foosball   1
2. Professional Foosball   5
3. Foosball Tables and Accessories   21
4. Foosball Terminology   27
5. Fundamentals of Foosball   31
6. Offensive Techniques   45
7. Defensive Techniques   78
8. Valuable Tips for the Advanced Player   90
9. Trick Shots   100
10. Game Variations   106

11 Common Rules and Etiquette   112
12 Tournament Competition   117
13 Women's Competition   130
14 Bridging the Communication Gap   133
    Appendix I: WTSA Rules of Play   135
    Appendix II: Money Winners, Championships,
            and Awards   152
    Appendix III: Professional Player Biographies   159
    Index   171

Acknowledgments

The author would like to thank the following people for their cooperation and contributions: Luc Mertens, Faye McWilliams, Joe McCarthy, Don Marshall, Cal Rogers, Lee Peppard, and the professional players who contributed information to this book. Most important, to my parents, for their invaluable support.

Introduction

I began playing foosball in 1971 at the age of fifteen. At that time, there were no tournaments or incentives to play other than a love of the game. Never would I have dreamed of a career in promoting foosball, or of a million-dollar professional tour that would draw players from all over the world. Today these things are a reality. Within a decade, foosball has been transformed from an arcade or barroom diversion into a sophisticated, professional sport, with organized competition and prize purses as large as those in golf and tennis.

The first professional foosball tour, held in 1975, gave top players from different parts of the country the opportunity to travel and compare styles and theories of play. At the start of the tour, regional styles varied greatly and the rivalry among players from certain areas of the country was intense. By the end of that first tour, however, a group of top players whose skill level had progressed enormously emerged. No longer was their style of play regional, as in "slow Texas style" or "Portland rocketball"; rather, it reflected a combination of the best techniques found nationwide, which were tested on the tour and could only be called professional.

These first professional players were true pioneers, not because they were traveling on the first professional foosball tour, but because they were actually *creating* the basic fundamentals of the sport as players know it today. No limits were placed on the imagination used in the search for the unstoppable shot or the impenetrable defense. The element of surprise was of tremendous importance, and the first pros were often reluctant to share their accumulated knowledge and their secret weapons.

As the faces across the table at tournaments became more and more familiar, the element of surprise lost some of its effectiveness. Through a process of natural selection, certain techniques became standard parts of a player's repertoire. The emphasis shifted from surprise to finesse, and it was natural for players to become more open and more willing to share their knowledge with others. Today, what separates the professional player from the amateur is the level of precision in the skills, which is achieved through dedication, practice, and tournament experience.

Professional tournaments have become a school of learning, not only for the pro players, but for the novice and rookie as well. Most professional players are more than willing to help another player, novice or pro, with some aspect of the game. Amateur players attending a professional tour event not only receive valuable exposure to professional competition, but are also able to attend, at no charge, clinics offered by the world's top professionals. In addition, competition is offered at all skill levels, which enables the beginning player to sharpen his skills by playing against others at the same skill level. I would venture to say that the beginner could learn more in one weekend at a tour event than in months of play at home or in local competition.

The object of this book is to bring you the knowledge of the pros, which until now was accessible only at tournaments. All of the knowledge I have gained during my years on the pro tour is included here, along with tips from other professionals on their individual styles and theories. Intended as a complete guide to the sport of foosball for the amateur player, this book places special emphasis on the fundamentals of professional play. But, no matter what your skill level may be, I feel certain that this book can give you greater insight into some aspect of your game. There is no set formula for success, but a firm foundation is an essential first step. This book will give you the information necessary to build that foundation, plus advice from the pros that will keep you going in the right direction.

This is the dawn of a new professional sport. Each year more players participate and more prize money is awarded. With the help of this book, a generous amount of dedication, and many hours of practice, you could be one of the superstars of tomorrow.

1
History of Foosball

Every time you say "foosball," you're putting a foot in your mouth—a German foot!

Foosball is the American corruption of *fussball* (pronounced the same), the German word for soccer—literally *foot* plus *ball*. While the sport has the more formal name of table soccer, to the American players who love it, it's foosball, or just foos.

Unfortunately, the origins of the game are not as easy to trace as those of its name. Like many games, it is quite possible that variations of foosball developed in different countries over roughly the same time period. Since organized soccer first entered the sports scene in the 1860s, the invention of soccer's table version can be safely dated sometime afterward, probably in the late 1800s. The earliest United States patent for a foosball table was registered in 1901, but it is generally agreed that foosball, like soccer, originated in western Europe.

A recent article in a Belgian magazine (*Le Soir Illustre*, No. 2471, November 1979, p. 26) stated that the inventor of the first foosball table was a Frenchman named Lucien Rosengart, who lived from 1880 to 1976. An employee of the Citroen automobile

2 THE COMPLETE BOOK OF FOOSBALL

Rare shot of play on the ancient "Greek" foosball table.

factory, he amassed a huge fortune through his inventive genius. He is accredited with the invention of the minicar, front-wheel drive, and the seat belt, to name a few, besides baby-foot, the original name for foosball.

One of the oldest manufacturers of foosball is a Swiss company called Kicker, located in Geneva. Its table is also called Kicker and has been so popular in Switzerland, Germany, and Belgium that the word has become generic: kicker is to these European players what foosball is to Americans.

In European countries as well as in the United States, foosball did not become widespread until after World War II. One popular belief is that foosball was invented to help rehabilitate war veterans. While not invented for that purpose, foosball has been used in rehabilitation with great success, especially in rebuilding hand-eye coordination. Today foosball also plays a role in social rehabilitation, being a part of the recreational programs offered by many state and federal correctional institutions.

American servicemen are responsible for another common belief, one that has haunted American players for a long time. After being stationed in Germany, servicemen have often come home with tales of German foosball players who are so incredibly good that they could beat any American. During our first years of professional competition in the early 1970s, the prevalence of this idea irked many dedicated American players. We were getting so good—how could they be better?

Competition in Europe, compared to the United States, has been organized for a long time. Belgium leagues, for instance, were organized as early as 1950. It wasn't until 1976, however, that the European leagues from different countries finally united to form the European Table Soccer Union (ETU) and competed against each other in the European Cup, now an annual affair. Unification is still a big problem for European players. There are many different table brands, and each country naturally prefers its own. The shape of the playing figures, the size of the handles, and the composition of the balls varies from brand to brand, making it difficult for players to switch from one to the other.

As good as the Europeans may be at their style of play on their own tables, the Americans have one thing that they don't: a pro tour with a million dollars in prize money. Foosball competition in Europe has remained on a very small scale in terms of prize money. With the introduction of the American table, players in Europe are being brought together, playing more and more on the American table and using the American rules. They have an incentive: the American prize money!

The $250,000 World Championships in May, 1979, welcomed the largest European delegation ever—thirty-six players from England, Ireland, Holland, Belgium, Germany, and Switzerland. Disagreements between Americans and Europeans were inevitable, and most disputes concerned the rules. Once an official and a translator arrived at a table, however, it was often discovered that communication was the only problem. By the end of the tournament, transatlantic friendships had been formed and the Europeans' skill at the table had won the respect of many American players.

Foosball is played all over the world. It can be found in the

Middle East, North Africa, South America, Australia, and Tahiti, as well as in Europe, the United Kingdom, and North America. Two foreign countries who recently expressed the desire to participate in American tournament competition are Argentina and Japan. Don't be surprised if you see teams from these two nations at the World Championships in the near future.

What lies ahead for foosball? This question can be answered in one word: *more*—more players from more countries, competing at more tournaments for more prize money. A recent study revealed that every week 1.9 million people play a game of foosball—in the United States alone. The cause of the phenomenal growth of the sport in the United States during the last decade is no secret: someone took foosball, the tavern game, and turned it into a big-money professional sport.

2
Professional Foosball

Unlike the game's European origins, which are difficult to document, the genesis of the professional sport of foosball is easy to detail. There can be no doubt that the man responsible for turning the tavern game into the pro sport that it is today is E. Lee Peppard, president of a firm called Tournament Soccer.

In the sixties, prior to Peppard's involvement with foosball, a few tournaments were being held in various parts of the country. These were usually local promotions sponsored by a tavern owner, but even at that time players were willing to travel quite a distance to take part in tournament competition, no matter how small the prize money. As sincere as these early efforts were, no one involved seemed to have the vision to organize large-scale competition, or the courage to put big money into the sport.

Lee Peppard is a man of both vision and daring. As the owner of the Eight Ball Billiards tavern in Missoula, Montana, he organized his first major foosball tournament in 1972 for a total purse of $1,500. It was an amazing success, with players traveling from Oregon, Washington, and Idaho to compete.

6 THE COMPLETE BOOK OF FOOSBALL

Lee Peppard, founding father of professional foosball.

Exactly one year later, on Memorial Day weekend in 1973, the second Northwest championships were held, once again at Eight Ball Billiards, but with some very important changes. The prize money had been increased to more than three times what had been given away the year before—an incredible $5,000! To accommodate the large number of participants expected, twenty-eight tables had been set up—but they were not the familiar German brand used the year before. Instead, the players were introduced to a brand-new foosball table—Lee Peppard's brand—called Tournament Soccer.

The first Tournament Soccer table, manufactured in Taiwan according to Peppard's specifications, presented a major structural change: the solid rod. Accustomed to the hollow rods of German tables, the players complained at first, then adjusted to the change and were convinced by the end of the tournament that the solid rod encouraged a more controlled and more powerful style of play. Still a standard feature on today's Tournament Soccer table, the solid rod has been a major factor in the development of the American professional style.

Even more important than increased prize money and the solid rod, however, was the change in Lee Peppard's motivation: the $1,500 tournament the year before was aimed at promoting his tavern business; the $5,000 tournament was designed to promote his Tournament Soccer table. This unique concept of product promotion through tournaments is the theme behind the success story of Peppard's seven-year-old company—a story that is an integral part of the history of professional foosball.

The next milestone on the road to the creation of professional foosball was passed one year later—as tradition now demanded—on Memorial Day weekend. The popularity of foosball had grown dramatically during that year, not only in the Northwest, but in other parts of the country as well. While such early foosball greats as Marcio Bonilla, Larry Folk, Joe Snider, and Jack Briggs were establishing themselves as the best in the Northwest, other regions were producing a few legends of their own, such as Tom Hansen and Billy Sumption of Minnesota, Mike Bowers of Colorado, and Gary Pfeil and Ed Whitesides of Texas. Gary Pfeil is often referred to as the first professional foosball player because of the high standards he set in performance, dress, and attitude long before rules were put into effect requiring players to meet such standards. These foosball pioneers and hundreds of other players from all over the United States met at the first national foosball tournament in May of 1974 at Elitch Gardens in Denver, to play for a total of $50,000 in prize money!

Once again the mastermind behind the tournament was Lee Peppard, and the event was billed as the Tournament Soccer International Table Soccer Championships. If $50,000 in cash seemed unbelievable to the players, the visual impact of seeing 144 foosball tables in one room was staggering! This was foosball, and it was the big time.

The anecdotes from that first Denver tournament have become a permanent part of foosball folklore. The tales tell of three-hour matches, spinning rods, and unstoppable wall passes—tales more true than exaggerated! It was a learning experience for both the participants and the tournament organizers, to say the least. There is a big difference between a $5,000 tournament and a $50,000 tournament, and despite months of planning and preparation by Tournament Soccer, confusion reigned. It was the first exposure to the solid rod for many players, and the first exposure for everyone to the remarkable differences among regional styles and rules. Dismay and disputes caused by foosball culture shock, however, soon gave way to excitement as the competition progressed. The surrounding amusement park lent to the festive atmosphere, and if a player grew sluggish between matches, he had only to go for a ride on the roller coaster, which proved to be quite an eye-opener.

The final match in open doubles ended at 5:00 A.M. Tuesday. The winners of that endurance test—the first national champions in open doubles—were Gordy Somekawa and Joe Purcell from Seattle. They took home $8,000, with second place and $5,000 going to Bill Sumption and Tom Hansen. The other big winners that weekend were: open singles—Mike Bowers, first, and Dale Fallon, second; mixed doubles—Gary Pfeil and Lori Schranz, first, and Jack Briggs and Karin von Otterstedt, second; women's doubles—Karin von Otterstedt and Vicki Chalgren, first, and Karen Waehlte and Marla Gibson, second.

Out of the chaos of that tournament emerged a nationwide solidarity among the players. The World Table Soccer Association (WTSA) was formed, the players' organization that still serves as the governing body of professional foosball and is responsible for the official rules of play and the regulations concerning dress code and conduct of players. John Gililland, a player from Texas, became the first WTSA president and editor of its official news magazine, *Foos Noos*. Each region of the country had its own WTSA representative who contributed to *Foos Noos* monthly reports on what was happening in the area. Although both WTSA and *Foos Noos* have undergone many changes during the years, they still meet the needs of foosball players today in many nations the world over.

Another alliance brought about by the Denver tournament was the partnership between Lee Peppard and Cal Rogers, a player and foosball promoter from Texas. By far the most intense rivalry at the tournament was between the group from the Pacific Northwest, who played at a lightning-fast tempo, and

Cal Rogers takes a final look at a special poster announcing United Kingdom tournaments.

the Texans, who preferred a much slower—but deadly—pace. Cal was an unofficial spokesman for the Texas delegation, and through his conversations with Lee regarding the need for standardized rules and tournament procedures, a friendship was formed that led to the addition of Cal Rogers to the Tournament Soccer staff. Texas joined forces with Montana at the new Tournament Soccer headquarters in Seattle, which became, after a few months of planning, the launching pad for the most daring foosball promotion ever—the 1975 Quarter Million Dollar Professional Foosball Tour.

In January of 1975, Tournament Soccer announced the thirty-two cities that had been chosen as sites for tournaments. From Boston to Los Angeles to Honolulu, the tour took foosball from coast to coast and then some, with prize money ranging from $1,000 to $20,000. The tour ran from January through August, with the 1975 International Tournament Soccer Championships taking place Labor Day weekend at the Regency Inn in Denver, for $100,000!

Operating without the aid of nationwide distributors, the Tournament Soccer crew—made up of Cal Rogers, Steve Blattspieler from Missoula, and Kyle Edie from Texas—often had to bring the tables in themselves, taking foosball into many areas in which it was totally unknown. Through rain, hail, sleet, and automotive breakdowns the show went on, in a different city every weekend for thirty-two weeks. Being dependent on the availability of hotel space, the tour could not always make a geographically logical progression; a glance at the schedule shows that the crew drove to and ran tournaments in the following cities, during one six-week period from February 22 to March 29: first Reno, then on to Madison, Wisconsin, then back to Houston, up to St. Louis, over to Atlanta, Georgia, then back to Tulsa, Oklahoma! Another three-week nightmare took place during the last three weeks of May, when the trusty crew traveled from Tampa to Portland, Oregon, then to New Orleans. Looking back today, it is generally agreed that the completion of that tour was nothing less than a miracle.

But completed it was, and the Tournament Soccer crew wasn't the only group of people traveling from city to city. If Tournament Soccer was a little foolhardy in undertaking such a perilous tour, the players who traveled on the Quarter Million Dollar Tour must have been plain crazy. They quit their jobs, forgot their studies, and left their families behind to take part in one of the greatest sporting adventures in history. For the most part they traveled by car and lived on what they won from week to week. By August an elite group had established themselves as the hottest players on the tour, including such early greats as Lane Hunnicutt and Steve Simon from Texas; Ed Tuhkanen, Guy Volgelbacher, Paul Daltas, and Dan Kaiser from Minnesota; Ken Rivera, Faye McWilliams, Gayle Harding, and the Perin brothers from Oregon; and all the others already mentioned, such as Pfeil, Sumption, Hansen, Schranz, Whitesides, von Otterstedt, and Bowers. These top players joined others from all over the country in Denver on Labor Day weekend, to see who would be the new national champions.

Besides the fantastic increase in prize money, other changes were instituted at the second Denver nationals. Excitement ran as high as ever, but the carnival atmosphere of Elitch Gardens had been replaced by the class of the Regency Hotel. Eight months of tournament experience had led to the development of systematic tournament procedures, making it possible for the tournament to be run much more smoothly and efficiently than the year before. Regional rivalries were still intense, as they are today, but the WTSA rules, like the solid rods, had been established on a national level, eliminating much of the bickering that had existed the year before.

Dan Kaiser and Ken Rivera became foosball's first superstars, winning first place in open doubles—and $10,000 each! Second place went to Mike Belz and Brent Bednar, two high school students from Minnesota who proved then and there that they had a future in foosball. First place in singles went to Steve Simon, with second going to another young Minnesota player who was to be heard from again—Doug Furry. Mixed doubles went to Billy Sumption and Karin von Otterstedt, and Karin teamed up with Lori Schranz to win women's doubles. The top five money winners of the Quarter Million Dollar Tour were: Dan Kaiser, $14,160.00; Ken Rivera, $11,145.00; Johnny Lott, $8,362.00; Mike Bowers, $7,287.00; and Karin von Otterstedt, $7,057.50. Yes, people were making a living playing foosball!

Tournament Soccer capped off that weekend in Denver by announcing its plans for 1976: the $375,000 Tournament Soccer Spectacular. This tour was the first attempt at a twelve-month schedule—a full year of foos. Although there were fewer tournaments, the prize money had increased and there were now no tour tournaments for less than $5,000. The West Coast tour consisted of six tournaments held during the months of January, February, and March. Then the tour swung to the East Coast for seven tournaments, coming back to celebrate the Fourth of July in Portland, Oregon. The national championships were held once again on Labor Day weekend, but this time in a city that was fast becoming one of the major centers for foosball in the country: Minneapolis.

This $125,000 tournament, billed as the 1976 world championships, was one of the shining moments in the history of foosball. The beautiful Radisson South was by far the most elegant location yet to host a foosball tournament. The grand ballroom, with 200 foosball tables, was magnificent. With the player's dress code more strictly enforced than ever, the entire operation had an air of professionalism never before achieved. Sections of bleachers in the pit area made it possible for a very enthusiastic crowd to watch the important matches.

Pandemonium broke loose when the hometown boys, Brent Bednar and Mike Belz, runners-up the year before, defeated Marcio Bonilla and Jim Zellick (Montana) for first place in open doubles. Dan Kaiser, 1975 doubles champion, defeated defending champion Steve Simon to take first place in open singles. First place in mixed doubles went to Rick "Redeye" Beberg (California) and Bev Froom (Oregon), and once again Karin Gililland (formerly von Otterstedt) and Lori Schranz took first in women's doubles. A rousing awards ceremony followed the finals, and everyone stayed to applaud the champions.

Since the 1976 World Championships, the Radisson South in Minneapolis has hosted three other major tournaments: Super Singles in 1977, Super Doubles in 1978, and the 1979 World Championships. Each one was a tremendous success, but none has quite outshined the splendor of that Labor Day weekend in 1976, when foosball players looked around them and marveled at the progress of their sport.

Five more tournaments took place in the fall of 1976, and the tour moved into the new year without even breaking stride. The 1977 Tournament Soccer Spectacular was bigger and better than ever, offering foosball players a total of $500,000! Again, fewer tournaments were scheduled, but more prize money was offered, so that players' traveling expenses were reduced and a few more players could join that prestigious group who make their living by foosball alone. The 1977 tour introduced a new and exciting concept in tournaments with the $50,000 Super Singles. The hometown spell held true one more time at the Radisson as Doug Furry took first place and drove away with a 1977 Porsche 911 Targa! But it wasn't easy. Doug had to defeat the top players in the open singles category, including names like Simon, Bowers, Kaiser, and second-place finisher Mark Scheuer (also from Minnesota), then go on and play against the first-

The largest single prize to date, a 911 Porsche valued at $20,000, won by Minnesotan Doug Furry.

1977 $250,000 World Championship finals (left, Scheuer-Alwell; right, Jackson-Loffredo).

place winners from novice, championship women's, and novice women's singles in a handicapped playoff. Doug went on to become the leading money winner on the 1977 tour, with a year-end total of $25,190.

The 1977 World Championships offered an unprecedented $250,000 in prize money. Held November 3-6 at the Gateway Convention Center in St. Louis, this tournament provided foosball history with its biggest surprise ever: after paying their dues for three years on the pro tour, the corps of traveling professionals and top money winners watched two youngsters who were unknown on the pro tour beat the best and go home with the biggest prize money yet offered at one tournament—$12,500 each! Todd Loffredo and Gil Jackson from Colorado became foosball superstars, at the ages of seventeen and eighteen, respectively. Both Todd and Gil have proven that it was no fluke by continuing to be two of the top money winners in foosball today.

Other national title winners that year were Rick Martin (Idaho) in open singles, Steve Simon and Gayle Harding in championship mixed, and once again Karin Gililland and Lori Schranz in championship women's doubles.

The next tour was extended to last eighteen months, running from January, 1978, to May, 1979, and the prize money was increased to a fabulous one million dollars! One of the highlights was the $100,000 Super Doubles at the Radisson, where the Minnesota dynasty reigned once more, with Doug Furry and Jim Wiswell winning the super first-place prize: two new Corvettes! The $25,000 "Fun In The Sun" in Los Angeles celebrated both the Fourth of July and Tournament Soccer's fifth birthday with a players' party and poolside antics at the Pacifica Hotel. The $100,000 Chicago Classic was the outstanding tournament of the fall, at which record crowds witnessed two history-making events: European players of professional caliber competed in the United States for the first time, and Tom Spear and Shawn Coonrod, one of the most successful teams of 1978, won first place in open doubles for $10,000 in cash.

The St. Louis $10,000 Masters Invitational held in March of 1979 introduced a new idea to tournament competition. Billed as

PROFESSIONAL FOOSBALL 15

1979 World Championship finals—a $44,000 match (left, Kaiser-Spear; right, Wiswell-Furry).

Tournament Soccer's First Five Years

1973
$5,000 Northwest Table Soccer Championships
May 27–29, 8-Ball Billiards
Missoula, Montana

1974
$50,000 International Table Soccer Championships
May 22–27, Denver, Colorado

PRESENTS
THE **$50,000.00** INTERNATIONAL
"TOURNAMENT SOCCER™" CHAMPIONSHIPS

MAY 25, 26, 27, 1974
DENVER, COLORADO
OPEN DOUBLES & SINGLES
MIXED DOUBLES
WOMEN'S DOUBLES

Breakdown of Prize Money
OPEN DOUBLES $30,000.00 – 32 PLACES
OPEN SINGLES $12,000.00 – 32 PLACES
MIXED DOUBLES $4,000.00 – 16 PLACES
WOMEN'S DOUBLES $4,000.00 – 16 PLACES

Entry Fees
ONCE A PLAYER HAS QUALIFIED FOR THE $50,000.00 INTERNATIONAL TOURNAMENT SOCCER™ CHAMPIONSHIPS THE ENTRY FEES ARE AS FOLLOWS: OPEN DOUBLES – $25.00 PLAYER, OPEN SINGLES – $15.00 PLAYER, MIXED DOUBLES – $10.00 PLAYER, AND WOMEN'S DOUBLES – $10.00 PLAYER

Play at the **$50,000.00**
INTERNATIONAL 'TOURNAMENT SOCCER™' CHAMPIONSHIPS
is limited to qualified players ONLY.

TO QUALIFY
Open Qualification Tournament – May 23 and 24, 1974 Denver, Colorado
Open Qualification Entry Fee – $5.00/player in each category
To Register – Check in prior to 9:00PM on May 22, 1974 AT
Tournament Headquarters — **CAPITOL PLAZA INN**
303 West Colfax Ave., Denver, Colorado 80204 • 303–292–9010

PLAY and PRACTICE on "TOURNAMENT SOCCER™" the $50,000.00 GAME

For Tournament Information Write — Mountain West Recreational Supply, 7630 Occidental Avenue South, Seattle, Washington 98108 or call (206) 767-4792

1975
Quarter Million Dollar Tournament

Jan. 4 & 5
Seattle Center North Court
Seattle, Washington $2,000

Jan. 11 & 12
Sheraton Inn, 1400 Austin Hwy.
San Antonio, Texas $2,000

Jan. 18 & 19
Ramada Inn, 999 S. Main St.
Salt Lake City, Utah $2,000

Jan. 25 & 26
Denver Mechanize Mark
Denver, Colorado $5,000

Feb. 1 & 2
Ramada Inn, 1150 S. Beverly Dr.
Los Angeles, California $1,000

Feb. 8 & 9
Ramada Downtown, 401 N. First
Phoenix, Arizona $2,000

Feb. 15 & 16
Sheraton Inn, 5500 W. Kellogg
Wichita, Kansas $5,000

Feb. 22 & 23
Kings Inn, 303 West
Reno, Nevada $1,000

March 1 & 2
Sheraton Inn, John Nolen Dr.
Madison, Wisconsin $10,000

March 8 & 9
Ramada Inn, 381 S. Gulf Freeway
Houston, Texas $5,000

March 15 & 16
Ramada, 9636 Natural Bridge
St. Louis, Missouri $2,000

March 22 & 23
Ramada-Airport, 845 N. Central
Atlanta, Georgia $10,000

March 29 & 30
Sheraton Skyline, 6333 E. Skelly
Tulsa, Oklahoma $2,000

April 5 & 6
Lemmington Hotel, Downtown
Minneapolis, Minnesota . . $10,000

April 12 & 13
Ramada, Brice Road at 1–70
Columbus, Ohio $2,000

April 19 & 20
Olds Plaza, Downtown
Lansing, Michigan $2,000

April 26 & 27
Albert Pick Inn, 300 N. 2nd St.
Memphis, Tennessee $5,000

May 3 & 4
Hilton Inn, Beltway
Baltimore, Maryland $5,000

May 10 & 11
Ramada, Hwy. 70 at U.S. 1
Raleigh, North Carolina . . . $2,000

May 17 & 18
Ramada 1, Busch Blvd.
Tampa, Florida $2,000

May 24 – 26
Memorial Coliseum
Portland, Oregon $20,000

May 31 & June 1
Airport Ramada, Airline Hwy.
New Orleans, Louisiana . . . $2,000

June 7 & 8
Ramada Central, 70th at Grover
Omaha, Nebraska $5,000

June 14 & 15
Imperial 400, 125 Main
Rapid City, South Dakota . . $1,000

June 21 & 22
Finlen Hotel
Butte, Montana $2,000

June 28 & 29
Holiday Inn, Northwest
Indianapolis, Indiana $1,000

July 4 – 6
Ramada, DFW Airport
Dallas, Texas $20,000

July 12 & 13
Ramada, Logan Field
Boston, Massachusetts . . . $1,000

July 19 & 20
Ramada, Culver City
Los Angeles, California . . . $5,000

July 26 & 27
Civic Center
Honolulu, Hawaii $1,000

Aug. 2 & 3
Hilton Inn, Oakland Airport
San Francisco, California . . $5,000

CHAMPIONSHIP WARM-UP
Aug. 23 & 24
Stardust Hotel
Las Vegas, Nevada $10,000

FINAL QUALIFICATION TOURNAMENT
Aug. 27 & 28
Regency Inn Coliseum
Denver, Colorado . . . . Qualifier

1975 INTERNATIONAL TOURNAMENT SOCCER CHAMPIONSHIPS
Aug. 29 – Sept. 1
Regency Inn Grand Ballroom
Denver, Colorado $100,000

1976
375,000 Tournament Tour

COAST TOUR

3 – 25
ac Airport Hilton
tle, Washington $10,000

3 – 15
ntown Hilton Inn
ver, Colorado $10,000

20 – 22
Webb's Townhouse
enix, Arizona $5,000

27 – 29
en's Way Hilton, Long Beach
Angeles, California $5,000

h 5 – 7
rmont Hotel, Berkeley
Francisco, California . . . $5,000

h 12 – 14
rks' Howard Johnson's
o – Tahoe, Nevada $10,000

COAST TOUR

h 26 – 28
rousel Inn
umbus, Ohio $25,000

2 – 4
raton-City Center
adelphia, Pennsylvania . . . $5,000

9 – 11
att House
any, New York $5,000

16 – 18
mada S.W. – Fenton
Louis, Missouri $25,000

23 – 25
port Hilton – Romulus
roit, Michigan $5,000

30 – May 2
rafft's Inn
gara Falls, New York . . . $5,000

7 – 9
raton Inn
ck Island, Illinois $10,000

SUMMER SPECTACULAR

July 2 – 4
Hilton Inn
Portland, Oregon $25,000

INTERNATIONAL CHAMPIONSHIP

Sept. 3 – 6
Radisson South Hotel
Minneapolis, Minnesota . . $125,000

FALL SCHEDULE

Oct. 22 – 24
Hilton Inn
Salt Lake City, Utah $25,000

Oct. 29 – 31
Bend Open
Inn of the Seventh Mountain . $5,000

Nov. 5 – 7
Los Angeles, California $25,000

Dec. 3 – 5
Birmingham Open
Holiday Inn $5,000

Dec. 10 – 12
Florida Sunshine Open $25,000

AND $25,000 IN REGIONAL
TOURNAMENTS

1977
500,000 Spectacular Tour

4
L Pro-Am Invitational
s Vegas, Nevada $5,000

4 – 6
ttle Kickoff
Tac Hilton $10,000

8 – 10
rtland Championship
eraton – Lloyd Center . . $25,000

27 – 30
per Singles, Radisson South Hotel
nneapolis $50,000

1 – 4
s Angeles Summer Spectacular
cifica Hotel – Culver City $25,000

t. 2 – 5
stern State Championship
rrousel Inn, Columbus . . . $25,000

t. 16 – 19
ouisville - Tournament Soccer Open
ouffer Inn, Louisville . . . $10,000

. 1 & 2
lbany New York Open
lbany Thruway House . . . $10,000

Oct. 28 – 30
Chicago AMOA Special
Playboy Towers $10,000

– AND –
$ 250,000 WORLD CHAMPIONSHIPS
November 3 – 6
St. Louis, Missouri
(and $100,000 in Regional Tournaments.)

1978-79
One More Million

Jan. 13 – 20
NFL Invitational
Tampa, Florida $5,000

Jan. 20 & 21
Player Appreciation Bash
Sahara Tahoe

Feb. 3 – 5
Seattle Kickoff
Children's Orthopedic Hospital Open
Seattle Center
Snoqualmie Room $10,000

Feb. 10 – 12
Schlitz & Amusement Unltd. Open
Eugene, Oregon $10,000

Feb. 17 – 19
Time Zone, California
Santa Cruz Holiday Inn . . . $10,000

Feb. 24 – 26
Salt Lake City Open, Hilton Inn
Salt Lake City, Utah $10,000

Banner Specialty Open
Quality Inn – Pentagon City
Arlington, Virginia $5,000

March 3 – 5
Pinball Wizard Open
Palmer Auditorium
Davenport, Iowa $10,000

N.E. Tournament Soccer Spectacular
Whimsey's at Copley Plaza Hotel
Boston, Massachusetts $5,000

March 10 – 12
Shaffer Distributing Open
Ohio $10,000

March 24 – 26
A.C.U.I. Open, Marriott Hotel
Rochester, New York $50,000

April 7 – 9
SRB Distributing Open
Parliament House
Birmingham, Alabama . . $10,000

April 14 – 16
Feyline Open, Harvest House Hilton
Bolder, Colorado $10,000

April 27 – 30
Northwest Open, Exposition Center
Portland, Oregon $50,000

May 19 – 21
Indianapolis Vending Open
Stouffer's Hotel
Indianapolis, Indiana $10,000

May 26 – 29
Super Doubles
Radisson South Hotel
Minneapolis, Minnesota . . $100,000

July 1 – 4
Tournament Soccer
5th Birthday Party
Pacifica Hotel
Los Angeles, California $25,000

July 22 – 24
St. Louis Classic, Strafford House
Fenton, Missouri $10,000

July 28 – 30
Toronto Open, Howard Johnson's
Toronto, Canada $2,500

Aug. 4 – 6
Calgary Open, Pallister Hotel
Calgary, Alberta $2,500

Aug. 11 – 13
Vancouver Open
Sheraton Plaza 500
Vancouver, B.C. $2,500

Aug. 18 – 20
Edmonton Open, Regancy Hotel
Edmonton, Alberta $2,500

Aug. 25 – 27
Seattle Open, Olympic Hotel
Seattle, Washington . . . $10,000

Sept. 1 – 4
Portland Open, Hilton Inn
Portland, Oregon $20,000

Sept. 8 – 9
Spokane Open, Convention City
Spokane, Washington $5,000

Sept. 22 – 24
Louisville Open, Marriott Hotel
Louisville, Kentucky . . . $10,000

Sept. 29 – Oct. 1
Minnesota Open, Kohler House
Rochester, Minnesota $10,000

Oct. 29 – 31
Lake Geneva Classic, Interlake Inn
Lake Geneva, Wisconsin . . . $10,000

Nov. 10 – 12
AMOA Classic, Pick Congress Hotel
Chicago, Illinois $100,000

Nov. 25 – 27
Recreation Warehouse Open
Niagara Hilton
Niagara Falls, New York . . . $10,000

March 8 – 10
Shaffer Distributing Spectacular
Drawbridge Inn
Cincinnati, Ohio $50,000

April 13 – 15
A.C.U.I. Open, MGM Grand Hotel
Reno, Nevada $50,000

AND
MEMORIAL DAY 1979
$250,000 WORLD FOOS FESTIVAL!

(AND MORE TOURNAMENTS
FOR 1979 TO BE ANNOUNCED.)

the Decathlon of Foos, this tournament consisted of twenty-three rounds of competition, including draw your partners, goalie wars, and singles events. The masters were required to register weeks before the tournament, allowing the charts to be completely predrawn. Players earned points in each round and the four players with the highest total of points played off to see who was the best all-around player in the world. The title, the glory, and $2,000 went to Todd Loffredo, with second place going to fellow Coloradoan, Tom Spear. The highest placing woman at the tournament, Carrie Crowell from Missouri, placed seventh in the overall competition.

The Masters Invitational was just the start of the special events that took place in the spring of 1979. The $50,000 Super Singles II took place in Cincinnati the second weekend in March. Dan Kaiser once again proved that he is one of the all-time best in singles by winning the playoffs and $5,000 cash. Then players traveled to Nevada to compete at one of the most spectacular locations to ever host a foosball tournament—the luxurious MGM Grand in Reno. Two old-timers—Mike Belz and Brent Bednar—took time out from Reno's distractions to play some serious foosball, winning first place in open doubles and $5,000.

Then it was back to the Radisson in Minneapolis for the 1978-79 World Championships, where Super Doubles winners Furry and Wiswell did it one more time, winning $15,000 each and the title of World Champions in open doubles. Also claiming the world champion title at that tournament—or reclaiming it, in this case—was Dan Kaiser in singles (his third national title, having won doubles in Denver in 1975 and singles in Minneapolis in 1976). Tom Spear set a precedent by being in the finals in all three championship categories. He teamed up with Kaiser to finish second in doubles, lost to Kaiser to finish second in singles, but succeeded in winning a world champion title with Carrie Crowell in championship mixed doubles. Carrie also took first place in championship women's doubles, playing with the top female money winner, Lori Schranz. The only real surprise at the tournament was the amazing way in which these remarkable world champions had been able to stay at the top

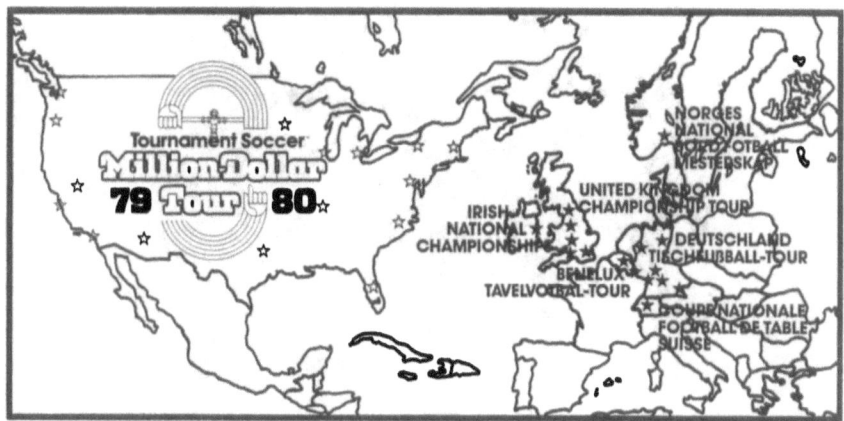

The 1979–80 Million Dollar Tour saw professional foosball go worldwide with tour events in seven European countries.

for so long, dominating the tour for the preceding few years, and in the cases of Schranz, Furry, and Kaiser, since the first tour in 1975. It's not easy to get to the top, but it's even harder to stay there.

The 1979–80 Million Dollar Tour II was back on the twelve-month schedule, from May to May. Highlighting the second Million Dollar Foosball Tour was the $250,000 East versus West World Championship playoffs. The first event in the playoffs, billed as the $100,000 World Championship-West, was held in Portland, Oregon, during the month of April. For those players who did not qualify in Portland, the tour proceeded to Chicago's glamorous Hyatt Regency for the $150,000 Eastern Division.

The winners from each division were guaranteed not only substantial first-place prize money (e.g., $10,000 for first-place doubles), but also a berth in the world championship playoffs. In one of the most exciting of all finals, the Eastern Division winners played off against the Western Division; one match, winner take all, for $50,000 in bonus money and the prestigious title of world champion. Victorious in the playoffs and the world champions for 1980 were: open doubles, Tim "Zeek" Burns and Mike Bowers; open singles, Johnny Lott; mixed doubles, Lori

1980 World Champions (left to right): Tim Burns—doubles, Herbert Perrin—highest European finisher, Johnny Lott—singles, Mike Bowers—doubles, Yvon Perrin—highest European finisher.

Schranz and Jim Wiswell; women's doubles, Lori Schranz and Carrie Crowell.

As the professional tour entered a new decade, it seemed appropriate that the world finals would feature many of the pioneers of the sport, such as Bowers, Froom, Burns, Wiswell, and Schranz. It's been quite a journey from the $1,500 tournament at Eight Ball Billiards in Montana in 1972, but thanks to Lee Peppard, Cal Rogers, and the Tournament Soccer staff, along with thousands of dedicated players, professional foosball is a reality.

3
Foosball Tables and Accessories

The first foosball tables to become popular in the United States were European—German, French, or Italian—with slick play fields. During the 1960s, thousands of these imported tables found their way into gamerooms, bars, and college student unions throughout the country. While those foreign tables would seem primitive by today's standards, they were widely accepted, and many of their playing features can still be found on today's professional table.

As foosball grew in popularity, American companies began to design and manufacture their own tables. Often using input from skilled players, each company strove to create the ultimate table with the best playing features, allowing versatility in shooting and optimum ball control. Several American brands of tables entered the market, each with its own playing characteristics. Some had wooden handles, while others had plastic; some featured slick balls and a slick play field, while others had textured balls and a rough play field. A player's favorite table was almost always the brand he could find in the local gameroom or bar. In those days, the mark of a good player was his

The Tournament Soccer table is the pro tour table.

or her ability to adjust to whatever table was being used at a tournament.

While a few manufacturers tried to promote tournaments, it was evident that a standard table was needed for nationwide tournament competition. The Tournament Soccer table has established itself as the standard tournament table through the Tournament Soccer pro tour.

However, several different brands of tables can still be found across the country, and there is a common belief among inexperienced players that all tables play the same. This is not true. There is a world of difference among the features and playing characteristics of different brands. The table you choose to play on and practice on should be the table that best meets your goals as a foosball player. If you are not interested in the serious competition of the professional tour but enjoy playing on the local level, you should naturally practice on the style of table that is predominant in your area. If you do want to learn the professional style of play with the goal of competing on the tour, you should definitely practice on the tournament table.

PURCHASING A HOME FOOSBALL TABLE

For a player who is serious about improving his or her game, it is a great asset to have a table at home for practice. When I started competing on the professional tour I felt that I had the edge on many of my opponents because I owned my own foosball table. As soon as I invested in my own table I noticed an immediate improvement in my overall game. For the first time I could practice shots and passes over and over again, until I had not only mastered the moves but had also become confident that I could perform them under tournament conditions. Intrigued by the unlimited possibilities on a foosball table, I was soon practicing more than ever before, learning techniques I had seen others use and inventing some of my own. I became a more consistent player and developed confidence and a positive attitude, both of which are essential steps in the development of a winner.

If you are dedicated to improving your foosball skills, the best possible procedure is to test your skills against local competition and then return home to your own table and work on the areas of your game that you know need improvement.

If you decide to purchase a home foosball table, keep your personal goals and needs in mind. Some manufacturers offer different models of home tables, ranging from a lightweight, inexpensive type to a durable model with playing characteristics identical to those of the coin-operated tables used at the professional tournaments. If you need advice, seek out an experienced player who can help you select the table that is right for you.

MAINTAINING YOUR FOOSBALL TABLE

In order to practice properly, you'll need to keep your home table in top condition. Perfect practice makes perfect! If you intend to raise your game to a competitive level, then you'll want play on your table to resemble play on tournament tables as closely as possible. Given proper attention, your table can be kept in tournament condition with a minimum amount of care.

24 THE COMPLETE BOOK OF FOOSBALL

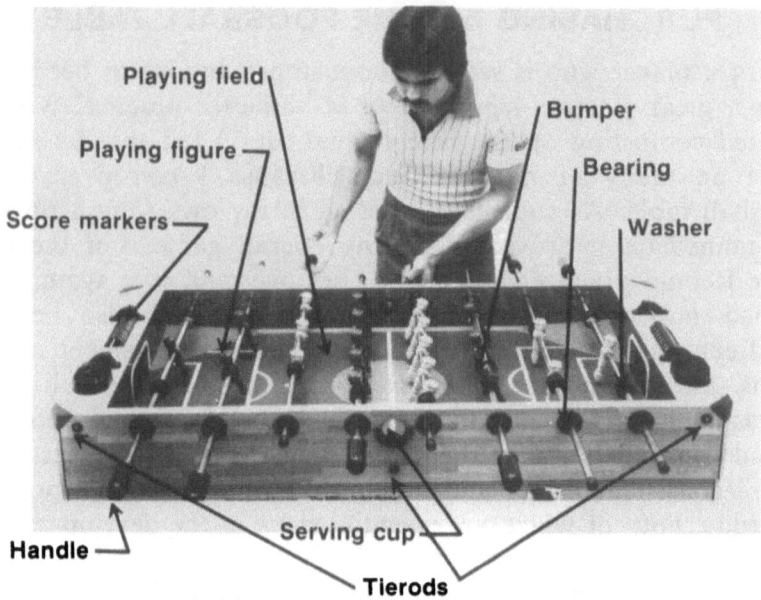

Components of a foosball table

While table maintenance may vary for different brands, the following tips are applicable to most tables and recommended for tournament tables. Use the picture below as a reference guide to assembling and maintaining your table.

Proper Assembly

Check the following components when assembling your table.

Handles. Be sure the handles do not slip and turn independently of the rods. If they do, this may be remedied by spraying the inside of the handles with spray paint (to make it sticky) or by putting tape on the end of the rods.

Playing figures. Be sure the playing figures are bolted on tightly; this helps prevent breakage.

Washers. Be sure the plastic washer is on the outside of the bumper (near the wall) and that the smooth edge of the washer is on the outside. The thin metal washer goes on the inside of each bumper (near the man).

Regular Maintenance

To keep your table in top playing condition, check the following details on a regular basis.

Lubricant. The best product to use to lubricate the rods is a high-quality spray-on furniture wax. Use this often to keep the rods gliding freely, but be careful not to spray it on the play field—it will damage it.

Play field. To clean your play field without damaging it, use a clean cloth and lighter fluid.

Playing figures. Check to be sure they are tight.

Bumpers. Cracked or broken bumpers should be replaced.

Periodic Maintenance

The following items should be checked every two to three months.

Bearings. These should be cleaned. A business card wrapped around the rod and twisted up into the bearing works well to remove built-up dirt and lubricant. Occasionally, a rod will slide very slowly even after cleaning and spraying with lubricant; this usually indicates that the bearings should be rotated. Simply remove the bearing, rotate its position, and retighten.

Balls. For best playing conditions, balls should be replaced periodically.

Playing figures. A clean cloth and a good all-purpose cleaner may be used to clean dirt built up on the toes of the playing figures; a steel brush also works.

Tie-rods. These should be checked for tightness; a loose tie-rod can quickly ruin a table. Also check leg bolts for tightness.

Accessories

Grip products. Foosball players often use aids to improve their grip. The majority of serious competitors wear gloves on one or both hands to ensure the best possible grip on the handle. A good quality golf or tennis glove works well, and gloves made especially for foosball are also available. Not

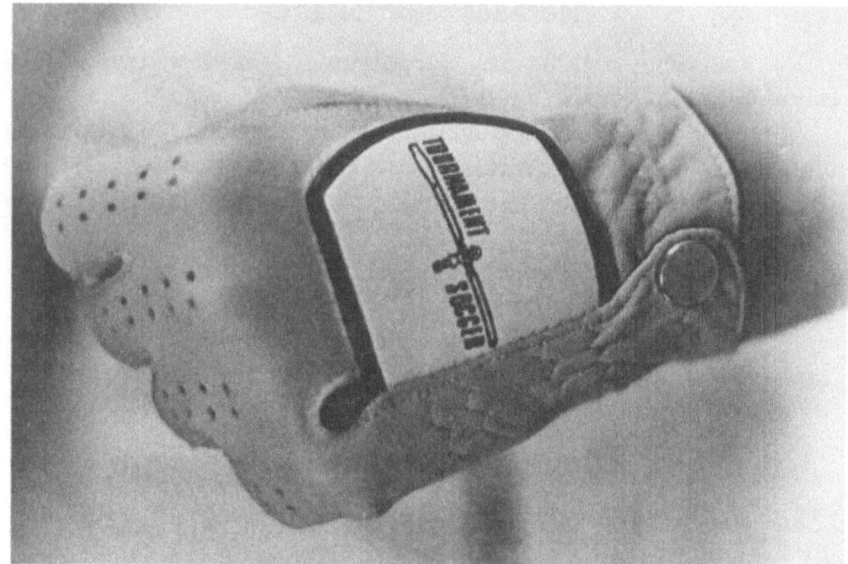

Practically every serious fooser uses a glove (or some type of grip product) to improve upon the grip.

everyone likes to wear a glove, but a good grip is important. Often a beginning player will notice an immediate improvement in his or her game by wearing a glove.

Some players prefer grip products, such as rosin, to keep their hands dry during competition. Two popular products used by players are grip cream and powdered rosin, applied directly to the hand. Both may be purchased at your local pro shop or sporting goods store.

Goalie booties. These leather strips are a must for every goalie. They are used to hold up the three- and five-man rods so you can practice goalie shots or play a game of goalie war.

Visors. Visors are great for the player who has trouble concentrating; many players swear by their visors and won't compete without them.

Table cover. This keeps your table free of dirt and dust.

Clothing. Foosball T-shirts, sweatshirts, jackets, belt buckles, and caps are all available—let the world know that you're proud to be a fooser!

4
Foosball Terminology

Before you can understand the advice offered by this book and by other players, you need to know some foosball terms. The following general terms are commonly used by players all over the country when discussing their favorite pastime. An understanding of the argot of foosball will automatically make you a better player by enabling you to make the most of your observations, readings, and conversations with other players.

Bail: when a player on defense overreacts, causing his playing figures to jump too far out of the way, thus missing the ball.
Bait: when a player on defense tries to trick the opponent into shooting the shot he wants him to shoot, usually by letting the opponent see an opening in the defense, only to close it as he shoots.
Between: used to describe one of the options in a series of shots, where the ball travels through the center section of the goal area and splits the two defending playing figures. Also called *split* and *middle*.

Camp: a type of defense in which the player completely takes away one of the opponent's shots or passes by keeping a playing figure consistently positioned, or camped, in that place.

Deadman: a type of shot that goes as far as possible, thereby going around the front playing figure when it is extended as far as it can go in the same direction as the shot (as in *to go deadman*, or *to shoot a deadman*). This is very difficult.

Double: to win first place in two events at the same tournament.

Draw Your Partner (DYP): a doubles tournament in which partners are picked by a random draw.

Drill: to score a very high percentage on someone (as in *he got drilled*).

Drop: the serve; to serve the ball.

Far: used to describe the opposite side of the table (*the far wall, a far-wall bank*), or the opposite side of the goal area (*he aimed for the far hole*).

Game Point: See *Meatball*.

Get Down: a slang term meaning to play as hard as you can.

Gut: the middle section of the playing surface, running from goal to goal (*the goalie shot straight down the gut*).

Hole: used to describe the part of the goal at which a player shoots (*the long hole was open*).

In-and-Out: a shot that counts as a point even though, after going into the goal, the ball pops back out onto the play field. Also called *pop-out*.

Inside: used to describe the side of the table closest to the player (*an inside bank*) or the options in a player's set of shots that go behind or between the playing figures (as in *he has a good inside game*).

Kibitzing: coaching from the sidelines; such advice from spectators is illegal and can result in a technical foul.

Long: one of the three main options in a series of shots, the other two being *short* and *middle*, in which the ball travels the farthest distance laterally before being shot into the goal (as in *he has a fast long*). *To go long:* to shoot the long shot. *The long hole:* the area in the goal through which the ball must pass when the player shoots a long shot.

Meatball: the final and deciding ball when the game score is tied four to four. Also called *sweatball* or *game point*.

Middle: one of the options in a series of shots (see *Long*), in which the ball travels through the center section of the goal area. Also called *between* or *split*. *To go middle:* to shoot a middle shot. *The middle hole:* the area in the goal through which the ball must pass when the player shoots a middle shot.

Near: the same as *inside* when referring to the side of the table (as in *the near wall*, or *a near-wall bank*).

Nit: slang for a beginner.

Option: a variation of the strongest shot in the offense; however, it attacks a different hole.

Outside: the same as *far*.

Pick: See *Stuff*.

Pits: an area in the tournament room reserved for important matches, containing one or more foosball tables and bleachers for spectators (as in *playing in the pits*, *a pit match*, or *a pit table*).

Pop-out: See *In-and-Out*.

Razzle Dazzle: a flamboyant style of play using fancy maneuvers, trick shots, and precision ball control. Also called *Saturday Night Foosball*.

Reject: See *Stuff*.

Saturday Night Foosball: See *Razzle Dazzle*.

Set Position: the ball is not moving and is in a still position ready to be passed or shot.

Skunk: to beat the opponent without allowing him or her to score one point (as in *looks like a skunk* or *he got skunked*).

Spike: See *Stuff*.

Split: See *Between* and *Middle*.

Squib: See *Stub*.

Stub: to mis-hit a shot by bringing the playing figure down directly on top of the ball, causing it to go askew; a shot hit in this way. Also called *squib*.

Stuff: to reverse the direction of a shot by simultaneously blocking and hitting it, usually right back into the opponent's goal; a shot hit in this way. Also called *spike*, *pick*, or *reject*.

Sweatball: See *Meatball*.

Telegraph: to unintentionally inform the opponent of an upcoming shot or pass through some action on the table or through a body movement.

Triple: to win first place in three events at the same tournament.

Turnover: to lose possession of the ball to the opponent.

Whiff: to swing and miss the ball completely, or to hit it poorly off to one side, usually resulting in a turnover.

5
Fundamentals of Foosball

Beginners or novices tend to overlook or underrate the importance of the basic fundamentals, such as the serve, grip, stance, and swing. These fundamentals form the foundation which often determines the difference between average players and skilled players. By developing these techniques correctly, a player can improve his overall game at a more rapid pace and to a higher level of skill.

THE SERVE

A consistent serve is a must in every player's game. The rules state that the serving player may influence the roll of the ball, so long as his hand does not enter the play area.

There are two popular techniques used in serving the ball. The cup drop is the easiest to learn, but, for consistency, I recommend that you learn the finger serve, in which you use your finger to influence the drop of the ball. At crucial points, you want to be confident that your serve will fall to *your* five-row, not to your opponent's.

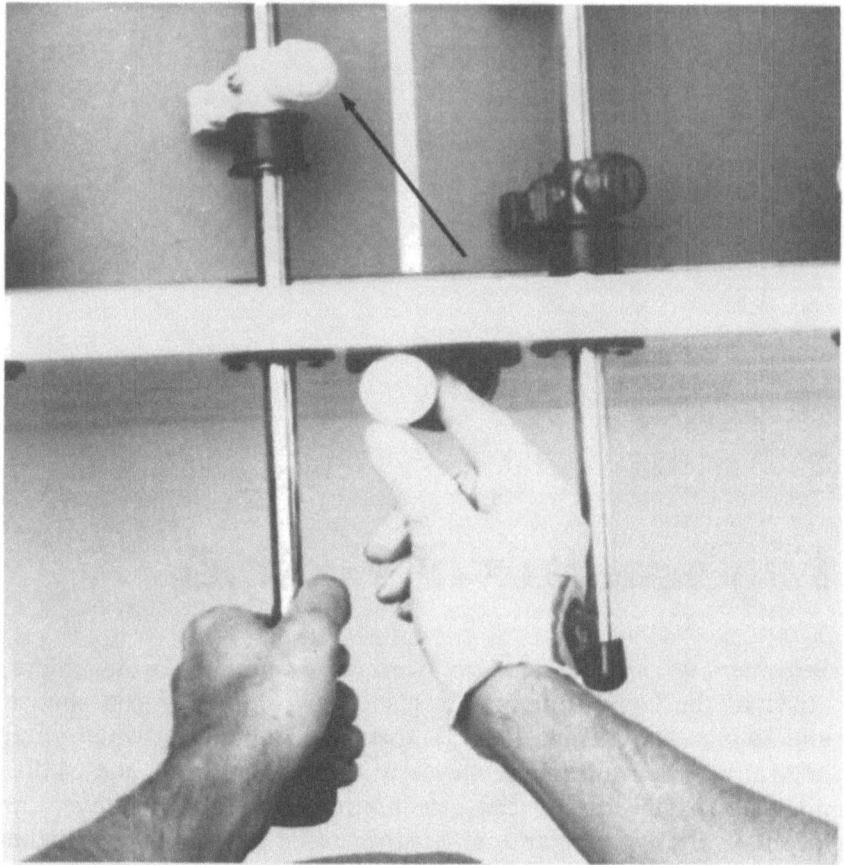

Figure 1: Cup drop serving method

Technique 1: Cup Drop Serve

A. Position yourself to serve the ball. Your left hand should be on the five-man rod, ready to gain control of the ball when it falls from the cup.

B. Now place the ball in your right hand and set it on the upper left-hand edge of the serving cup. When you release the ball, it should bank off the right inside wall of the cup and fall to your five-man line. You must be ready to gain control with the five-man, because the ball falls quickly with the cup drop technique. (See Figure 1.)

Technique 2: Finger Serve

A. Position yourself to serve the ball. Place the ball in the cup with your left hand. (It is permissible to reach into the play area in order to position the ball for the serve.) (See Figure 2.) Hold the ball in the upper right-hand corner of the serving cup.

B. Place the first finger of your right hand into the cup, to the left of and below the ball. Press up with this finger to hold the ball in place in the upper right-hand part of the cup, and put your left hand back on the five-man handle. Be sure this finger does not extend into the play area.

C. To make the ball drop toward your five-man, slowly release the pressure of your finger on the ball, allowing the ball to drop to the play field. For best control, do not pull your finger out of the cup until the ball has dropped. Simply press down, let the ball drop, then place your right hand on the three-man handle.

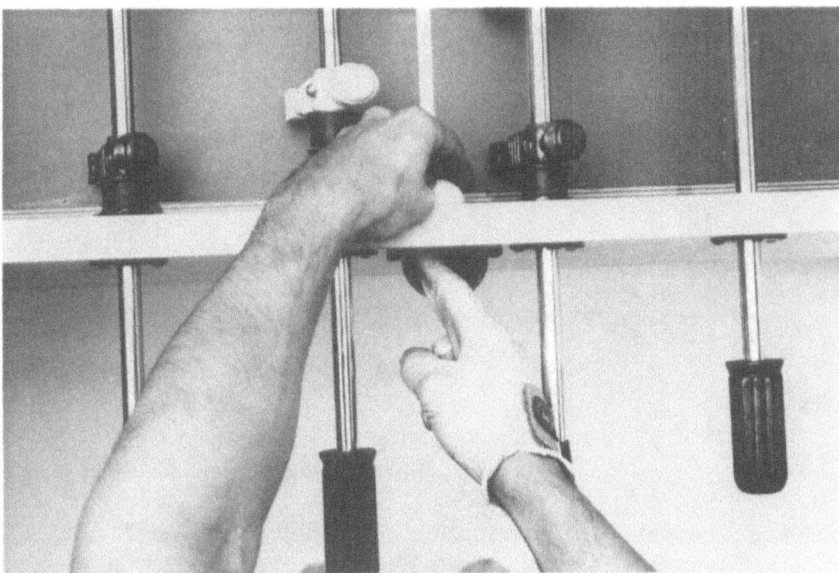

Figure 2A: Finger serve method

34 THE COMPLETE BOOK OF FOOSBALL

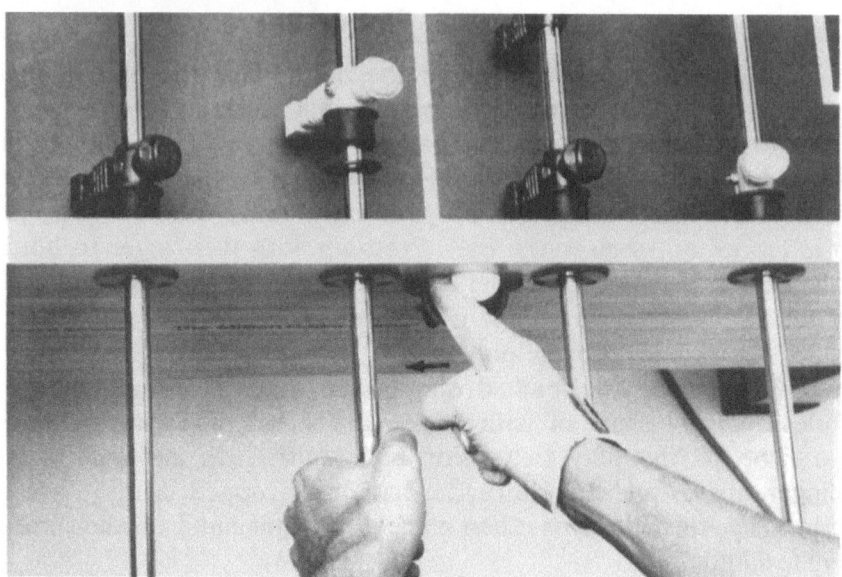

Figure 2B

Figure 2C

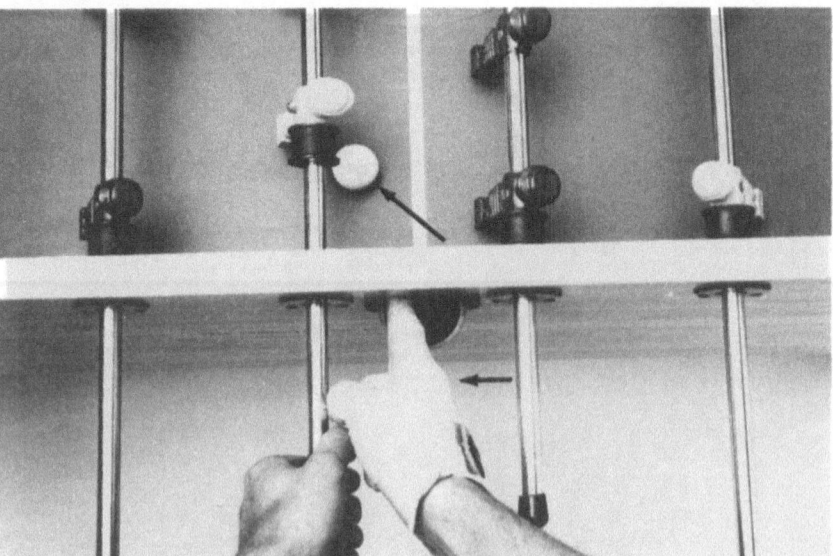

STANCE

A proper stance is a very important part of your game. The correct stance can mean more power on your shot, greater consistency, and added confidence under pressure. Sometimes a player will wonder why his shots are off goal, without realizing that he or she is standing differently than usual, playing in shoes of a different height, and so on. It may take a friendly observer to point out the difference the first time, but once you realize the importance of a consistent, well-balanced stance, it will become a natural part of the execution of your game.

No one can dictate which stance is best for you. You should feel comfortable in your stance so you can concentrate fully on your playing. Many players use one stance for overall play, but a different stance to shoot their set shots.

Technique 1: Flat-footed Stance

The following illustration shows the flat-footed, square stance. In this stance, you position your feet shoulder-width apart. Your weight is placed evenly on both legs and you stand squarely, facing the far right corner of the table. The flat-footed stance is a well-balanced stance for both forwards and goalies, and is used most commonly by players shooting pin shots, banks, and pull shots. (See Figure 3.)

Technique 2: Leg Back Stance

This versatile stance is probably the most commonly used stance among professional players, being popular with both pull shot and kick shot players. In this stance, you stand facing the table with your left foot placed approximately in line with your five-man rod. Your right foot is then placed eight to ten inches back, approximately in line with your three-man rod. Most of your weight is on the left foot, which is flat-footed. You stand on the toe of your right foot to achieve balance. (See Figure 4.)

36   THE COMPLETE BOOK OF FOOSBALL

Figure 3:
Flat-footed stance

Figure 4:
Leg back stance

Goalie Stance

The two stances discussed above can be used by both forwards and goalies. You may need to adjust your footing a little in the goalie position, remembering that it is most important to be comfortable and well balanced. The goalie should be sure to give his or her forward room to shoot. The following rule is a good one to play by: anytime the ball is in your forward's area, be sure to give him or her all the room needed, and when the ball is in your play area, your forward should reciprocate.

GRIP

When I started playing, the last thing that entered my mind was how to grip the handle. It just seemed natural. Hopefully, it also seems natural to you. However, if you're not getting the power on your shots that you would like, chances are the problem is in your grip.

There are three basic types of grips. The cannonball and the finger grip are used when hitting wrist shots such as a pull shot or pushkick. The third grip, the palm roll, is used mainly for bank shots and pullkicks.

I strongly recommend that beginners first learn how to shoot wrist shots. Developing a strong wrist will make you a more well-rounded player and improve your entire game in the long run.

Technique 1: Cannonball Grip

Probably the most common and most natural grip is the cannonball. It is simple to learn. First, get into your stance. Now wrap the palm of your right hand around the handle, with your thumb on the outside of your first two fingers. (See Figure 5.) In order to get a good release, grip the handle fairly tightly, but not too tightly or too loosely.

The cannonball grip is used by some of the most powerful pushkick and pull shot shooters in the world. It is also a good grip for backpins, squeeze shots, and push shots.

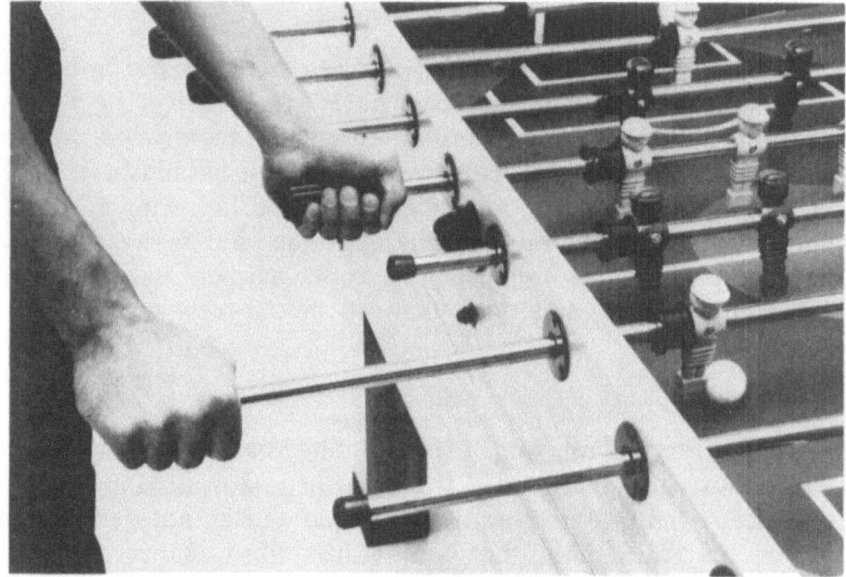

Figure 5: Cannonball grip

Technique 2: Finger Grip

Another popular grip for wrist shots is the finger, or golf, grip. This grip is more difficult to master than the cannonball, and unless it seems natural to you, I wouldn't recommend it for the beginning player.

First, get into your stance. Now place the lower half of your right-hand fingers and thumb on the handle. Your thumb and forefinger should be fairly tight, with your other fingers in a slightly looser grip. (See Figure 6A.) Your palm should not be touching the handle. In order to get a powerful release, you push through with your thumb as you snap your wrist downward. After the shot, your hand should be positioned as in Figure 6B.

Technique 3: Palm Roll Grip

A good palm roll is an important part of any player's game, as it is the most widely used grip for shooting bank shots. Most

FUNDAMENTALS OF FOOSBALL 39

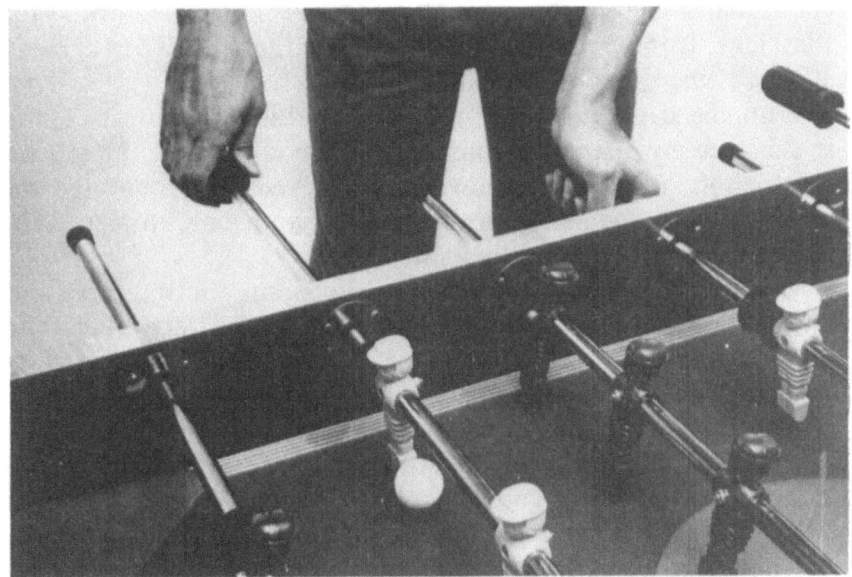

Figure 6A and 6B: Finger grip   (6A) Grip

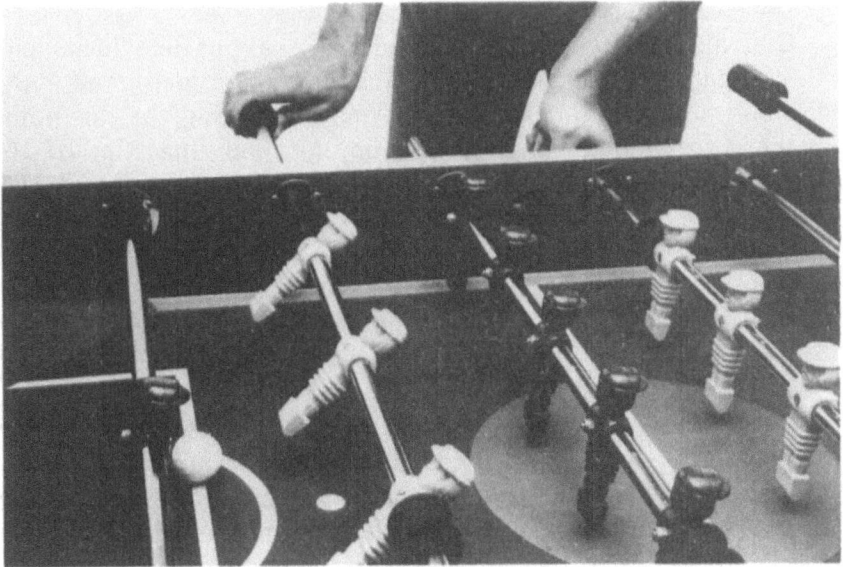

(6B) Followthrough

good goalies and good singles players excel in the palm roll grip. Pullkicks, frontpin shots, angle shots, and gut shots are all most effective when shot with a palm roll.

With the cannonball and finger grips, the power on the shots is achieved by snapping your wrist. Palm roll shots differ from wrist shots in that the power is achieved by smoothly and quickly rolling the handle in the palm of your hand to produce a powerful downstroke on the ball.

You should practice the palm roll by simply hitting a set ball directly into the goal. This way, you can concentrate on learning the grip. Once a powerful stroke is developed, you can work on using it to shoot banks, pullkicks, and many other shots.

A. Begin by gripping the handle in the cannonball style. Now lift your thumb from the handle. Your grip should now look similar to the one in Figure 7A.

B. You are now ready to address the ball. Using the middle playing figure on the three-man rod, position your man behind the ball, as in Figure 7A. Notice how the ball is positioned slightly behind the rod. This will help you get more power on the release.

C. Roll your hand down the handle about one inch. This should cause the playing figure's foot to rise an inch or so above the ball, as in Figure 7B. This is your backswing. At this point, prepare to catch the handle by cupping your fingertips. If you neglect to do this, your hand will slip off and cause you to spin the rod.

D. You are now ready to hit the ball. Applying a light pressure to the handle, quickly roll your hand upward until you catch the handle in your fingertips. This should cause the man to hit the ball into the goal; then follow through and end up positioned as in Figure 7C.

Keep working with the set ball until you consistently hit the ball hard. If you are having trouble, don't be afraid to experiment with different things. Try applying more pressure to the handle. Try a higher backswing or a deeper follow-through. Vary the speed at which you are rolling the handle. Stick with it and you'll soon be hitting the ball harder than ever before. Later in

FUNDAMENTALS OF FOOSBALL 41

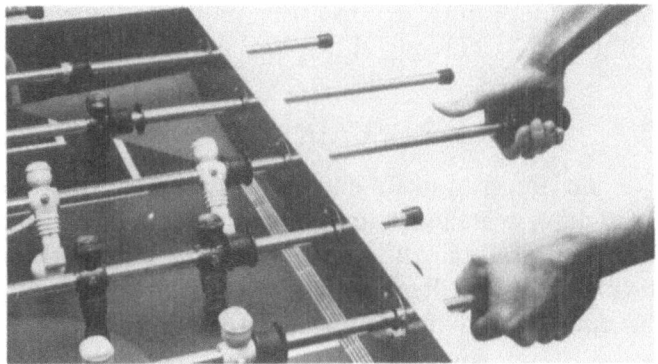

(7A) Grip

(7B) Backswing

(7C) Follow-through

Figures 7A–7C: Palm roll grip

the book, I will explain how to use the palm roll grip for shooting bank shots, pullkicks, pin shots, and more.

BALL RELEASE

Ball release is an important fundamental that can frustrate many beginners. I have watched many players attempt their first game of foosball and become discouraged because they lacked power when trying to score. Beginners often resort to spinning the rods because they can hit the ball harder that way.

A good release is not something that comes naturally. It is something that every player must develop through practice and play. It is mostly a question of proper timing.

First of all, you should have a basic knowledge of lateral speed. Lateral speed is the term used to describe the speed at which you pull or push the ball across the play field in order to be advanced by means of a pass or shot. In order to achieve a good release on the ball, your lateral speed should not only be quick but smooth as well. It should not be so fast that it becomes jerky. Many beginners feel they need to jerk the ball in order to get enough speed on the shot to score. This is not true. Most of the speed on a good shot comes from a powerful release, and in order to get a strong release, you must have lateral speed that is quick and smooth.

The next step in developing a good release is to use the proper backswing. Your backswing should be high enough for you to get a good position on the ball, yet not so high that you telegraph, or give away, the timing of your shot to the opponent. Position on the ball is very important. As you move the ball laterally, your backswing should cause the path of the ball to go slightly behind the rod. (See Figure 8A.) When you release the ball you will get more power and square off the ball better when the ball is positioned slightly behind the rod. This causes the playing figure to have a squeeze effect on the ball, therefore giving the shot more velocity. Be careful not to get the ball back too far—this will cause you to stub the ball between your man and the playing surface.

FUNDAMENTALS OF FOOSBALL 43

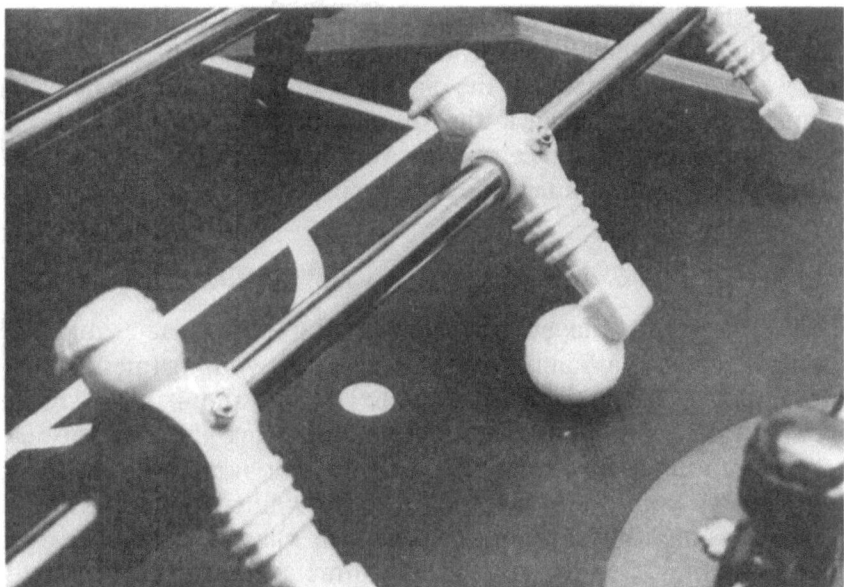

Figure 8A: Proper ball positioning

Figure 8B: Release and followthrough

The third and final step is a good follow-through. Once you have the ball in position and have begun your swing, you should carry the swing through the ball and end up positioned as in Figure 8B. Never neglect the follow-through. Address the ball with complete confidence and always finish the shot. The follow-through will add momentum to the ball.

OVERALL BALL CONTROL

No book—or player, for that matter—can teach you ball control. This very important aspect of your game can be developed only through much practice and actual play against competition. You should practice maneuvering the ball between every two men on the table, and in every possible position. Obviously, you don't want to do this while you're playing a serious game, but anytime you're just playing a lighthearted game among friends you should practice your ball control. Throw the ball around a little bit—shoot some razzle dazzle, maybe a bank from the three-man rod, or a pullkick if that's a shot you seldom use.

Have fun! After all, that's what foosball is all about. In the meantime, you'll be developing that added touch that will help you pick up the ball the next time it flies around the table on match point.

6
Offensive Techniques

At first glance, foosball seems like a simple enough game. However, after playing their first game, most people are amazed at how difficult it can be. Many times, out of the frustration of not being able to control the ball or advance it with any power, beginners will resort to random spinning of the rods, which is illegal. If you are a beginner and find it difficult to maneuver the ball or get off a shot with any power, you should not get discouraged. In over ten years of playing and teaching, I have yet to run across a person who has not had to deal with the same frustrations and learning stages as every other beginner.

Proper offensive techniques are not developed overnight. Be patient. Take it one step at a time and always be analyzing your progress and working to improve upon any weaknesses.

In order to describe certain maneuvers, it will be necessary to refer to specific playing figures and rods on the table. For ease of reference, use the numbering system illustrated in the picture below.

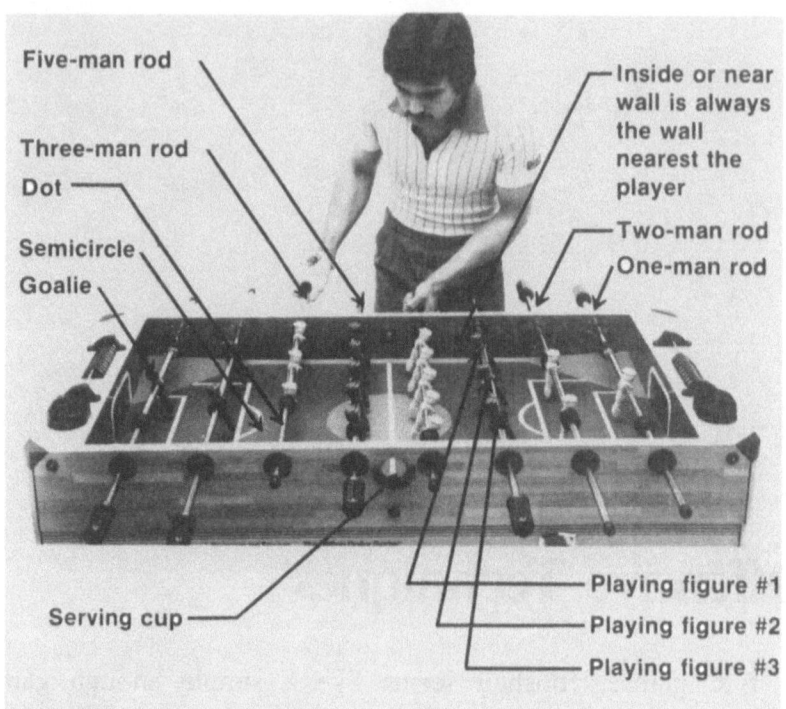

FORWARD POSITION

Passing from the Five-Man to the Three-Man

A strong forward game requires proficiency in passing from the five-man line to the three-man line. Most shots are scored from the three-man line. Shots from this line yield the highest percentage of points because, obviously, this line is closer to the goal than the five-man line, and it has fewer defensive playing figures which the ball must pass through. However, the most powerful shot on the three-man is of no value if the forward cannot get the ball there to shoot it. The importance of a good passing series has grown immensely in the last few years on the tour. Today, the outstanding difference between a pro forward and a beginning forward is the ability to pass the ball from the five-man to the three-man line.

A few of the more popular passing series follow. You will notice that most of these passes entail using your inside no. 1 and no. 2 men on the five-man row. While many other combinations using the other playing figures are possible, your percentage passing series usually involve these two playing figures and work the three-inch area off the inside wall.

TECHNIQUE 1: THE FAST WALL PASS

The fast wall pass is a basic maneuver that should be easy to learn. Begin with the ball positioned on the inside of your no. 2 man on the five-man line. Next, using the no. 2 man, quickly advance the ball toward you to the wall. (See Figure 10A.) As soon as the ball makes contact with the wall, your no. 1 man should be positioned directly behind the ball and ready to hit the pass. (See Figure 10B.)

Once the ball reaches the wall, advance it with your no. 1 man to your no. 1 man on the three-man line. With a little practice, you can hit this pass to the wall very quickly.

TECHNIQUE 2: THE STICK PASS

The stick pass is an option to the wall pass. Using the same maneuver as described for the fast wall, pass the ball about an inch away from the inside wall in the lane between the opponent's men. This works well when the opponent is camping his or her defensive man on the wall.

It is very important to have at least one option to each pass you use. The option should be executed at the same speed and in the same manner as the main pass, but it should attack a different hole in the defense. For instance, a good wall pass will be ineffective without the right option, such as the stick pass.

48 THE COMPLETE BOOK OF FOOSBALL

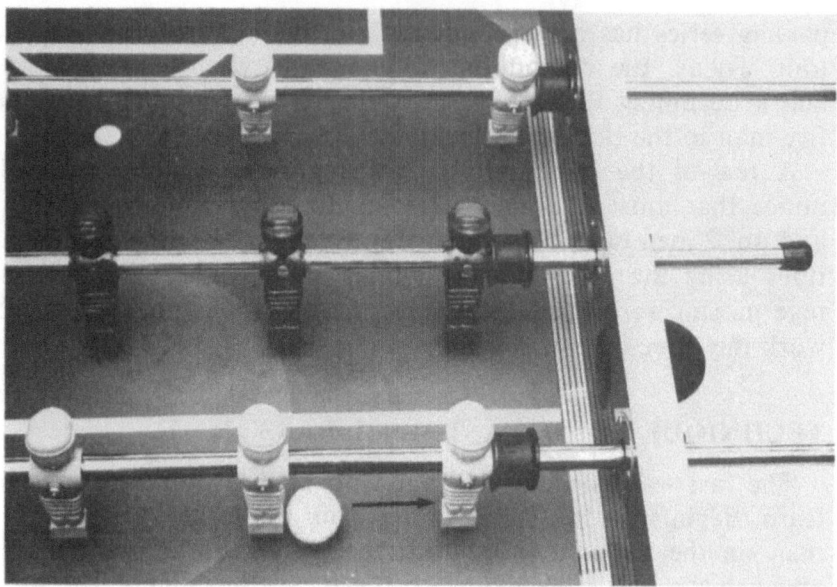

Figures 10A and 10B: Fast wall pass

TECHNIQUE 3: THE ANGLE-UP PASS

Begin with the ball positioned on the inside of your no. 2 man of the five-man line. Smoothly advance the ball toward you at about medium speed. Your no. 1 man should be positioned against the wall as the ball approaches. (See Figure 11A.) As the ball reaches your no. 1 man, you should hit it so that it angles upward (toward the center of the table), through the lane of your opponent's men.

There are two different ways to hit the angle-up pass. The chip angle-up is done by bringing your no. 1 man down, chipping about one-third of the ball. The chip should put enough speed on the ball that when your opponent bails to the wall he does not have time to react, come back, and stop the pass.

The scoop angle-up is one of the most popular, and definitely one of the most effective, passes used by the pros. It's not difficult to learn, but it takes practice to become consistent with it.

As the ball is advanced from your no. 2 man to your no. 1 man, it should move slowly and smoothly, and should roll slightly behind the rod. This is important, because if it is not slightly behind the rod, you will not get enough angle on the pass. Now, rather than quickly chipping the ball, swing through it with a scooping motion. The key to this pass is not speed, but smoothness.

TECHNIQUE 4: THE ANGLE-DOWN PASS

An option to the angle-up pass (also called an uphill pass), is the angle-down, or downhill, pass. Begin exactly as you would to do an angle-up. When the ball reaches your no. 1 man, swing down through it, scooping it at an angle toward the wall. (See Figure 11B.)

Pro Tip on the Five-Man—Todd Loffredo

Since many beginners try to develop their own style of passing, they often develop bad habits. As they improve,

50 THE COMPLETE BOOK OF FOOSBALL

Figure 11A: Angle-up pass

Figure 11B: Option-angle down

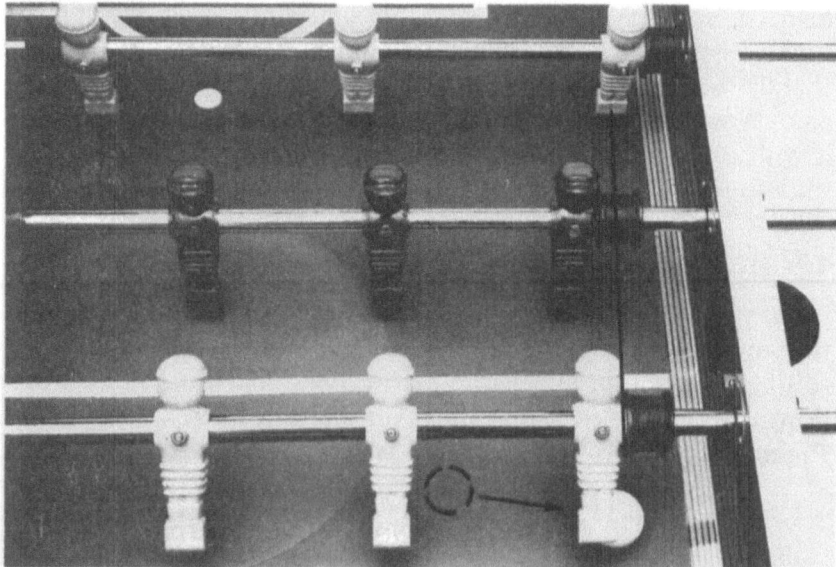

they realize that they must completely relearn the art of passing.

To prevent this, you should try to find a local player who has a strong passing game and then pattern your style after that player. When I first began playing on the tour, I picked out a specific pro whose passing style I liked, and I set out to copy his style. Soon I was passing as well as, maybe even better than, the player I learned from.

Variations on the Five-Man

I have explained some of the basic moves on the five-man line. However, there is no limit to the number of passes possible on a foosball table. By simply throwing in a hesitation, a fake or two, or by changing the lateral speed, you can throw off your opponent and increase your passing percentage.

A properly used fake can help you decide which option to use and, at the same time, confuse your opponent. Be sure your fake looks similar to the actual pass. If it does, it will cause your opponent to react as if you had passed the ball. By observing his or her reaction, you can increase your chances of selecting the correct option to use.

To position the ball slightly behind the rod when passing, many players begin by backpinning (positioning the ball between the man and the playing surface behind the rod) the ball with the no. 2 man on the five-man line. This helps with passes that emphasize smoothness, such as the angle-up and angle-down passes.

Don't forget to vary your lateral speed occasionally. This will throw off the timing of your opponent's defense.

Catching the Ball

Catching the ball is an art, just as is passing the ball. Before you begin to pass the ball, always check your three-man line. It should be positioned against the wall, and the men should be tilted forward. The men should be high enough so that the pass does not bounce off, yet not so high that the ball can roll underneath. If you do a pass in the lane, never move the three-man line until after the pass is hit. This way you won't telegraph your pass by the position of your three-man.

Shooting From the Three-Man

What's the number one shot in foosball? I can't begin to count the number of rookie and beginning players who have asked me that question. In order to give a thorough and objective answer, I decided to dig into the history books and let the facts speak for themselves.

As of this writing, a hundred tour events have been staged since the pro tour began in 1975. In the prestigious open doubles category, approximately 95 percent of the victories have been won by one of three basic shots—the pushkick, the pullkick, or the pull shot. A whopping 61 percent of the victories were attributed to players using a pull shot. The second highest rate of success was posted by players using the pushkick offense, which accounted for 20 percent of the first-place finishes. Another 15 percent of the wins can be accredited to players using the pullkick set. The remaining 4 percent were won by players using the pin shot offense.

Faced with these facts, many players might think that the pull shot is the most effective offense. However, if you compare the finals of the world and national championships, the statistics are much closer, with the pull shot accounting for 45 percent of the victories, the pushkick 39 percent, and the pullkick 16 percent. The main point I want to make about all this is that a professional player does not judge the effectiveness of an opponent by which shot he or she uses. Instead, the pro is more concerned with the opponent's effectiveness in utilizing his shot. In other words, it doesn't matter if you prefer a pullkick, a pull shot, a pin shot, or a pushkick—what does matter is how proficient you are in executing the shot.

Basic Techniques and Options

The rest of this chapter will give you insight into the basic techniques and options involved in each shot. Decide which shot is most natural for you and make up your mind that you're going to become effective not only in the shot itself, but also in every option that goes with it. Practice hard, play against competition, and try not to become discouraged. Make the most of your practice time by analyzing your mistakes and working to correct them. Remember, perfect practice makes perfect!

TECHNIQUE 1: THE PUSHKICK OFFENSE

The first thing to do in order to score well with any offense is to develop a strong outside game. By outside game I mean that you need to have a strong, fast long shot—the one that goes around the opponent's defense and into the corner of the goal farthest away from the original placement of the ball. A smart goalie will usually begin by leaving you the long hole rather than the shorter and easier inside holes. If you can establish a smooth, quick long shot, then you will probably be able to work all the holes and score on a good percentage of your attempts.

To shoot a pushkick, begin by setting the ball directly under the rod and even with the inside white line. (See Figure 12A.) It is important that you set up the ball as close to this position as time allows on each and every shot. This will help you develop consistency.

Arrange the defense, as in Figure 12A, with the outside playing figure positioned even with the dot. This is called a crossover defense. This forces you to shoot long enough and yet leaves a hole large enough for you to score and become consistent.

Now make sure you are in the proper stance. You should feel comfortable and well balanced. Your first shots should be slow and smooth. Your concentration should be focused on getting a crisp, hard release. As you push the ball with the no. 1 man, try to keep it slightly behind the rod. This will help develop power

54 THE COMPLETE BOOK OF FOOSBALL

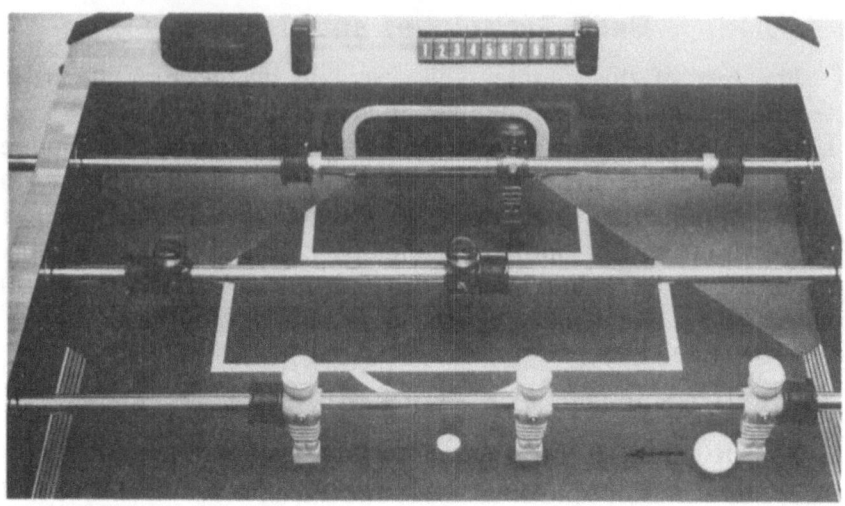

Figures 12A and 12B: Pushkick offense long shot

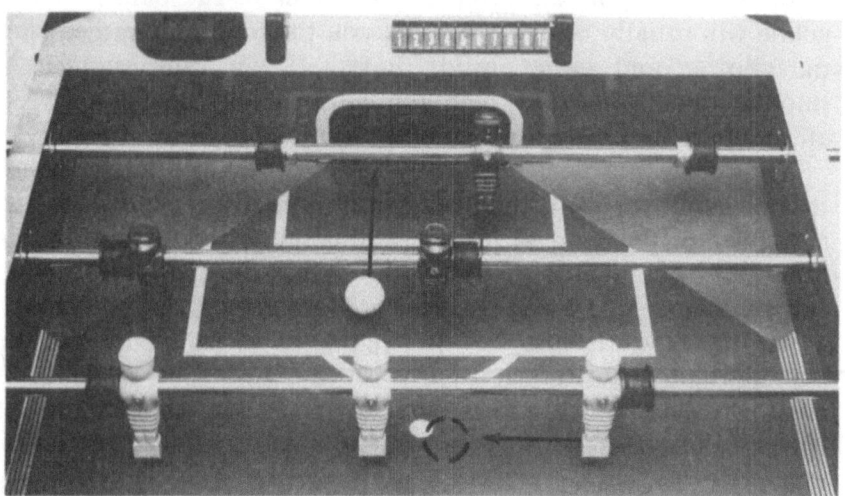

as you release the ball into the far hole with the middle playing figure. (See Figure 12B.)

Once you consistently hit the ball hard, try to start adding more lateral speed to the shot. Take it a little at a time and keep the shot smooth. Never jerk the ball. Continue to practice the shot on a still defense until you are able to hit it crisply into the goal with a fair amount of lateral speed.

At this point, you should begin learning the options to the pushkick offense. In order to be able to practice your long pushkick against different goalies, you must first have some type of inside game. By inside game I mean the options other than the long hole. By learning the basic dot shot, angles, and the dink shot, you will be able to work the different holes in a defense and develop your shot properly.

Pushkick Options

Dot Shot. The dot shot, or middle kick, is just the same as the long pushkick, except you release the ball over the center dot. The object is to score between the opponent's men in the defense. (See Figure 13A.) Shooting a pushkick, you are likely to come up against many race defenses. The dot shot, if shot at the same speed as your long, will cause the opponent to overrun the hole, therefore leaving the middle hole open.

Dink Shot. The shot that probably frustrates more goalies than any other is the dink. The dink is to foosball as the change-up or slow ball is to baseball. The object is to catch the opponent by surprise, which causes him to overreact or bail out of the hole.

Set the ball up and get into your stance. Now, what you are going to do is a push shot with your no. 1 man releasing the ball into the short hole. (See Figure 13B.) The key to making the goalie bail is to shoot the dink at the same takeoff speed as for your normal long shot, yet not as hard into the goal. Start the shot smoothly and quickly, as you would for the long shot. To avoid hitting the ball too hard, don't follow through as you normally do. Instead, stop your follow-through about halfway to three-quarters of the way through. A correctly hit dink is just

56 THE COMPLETE BOOK OF FOOSBALL

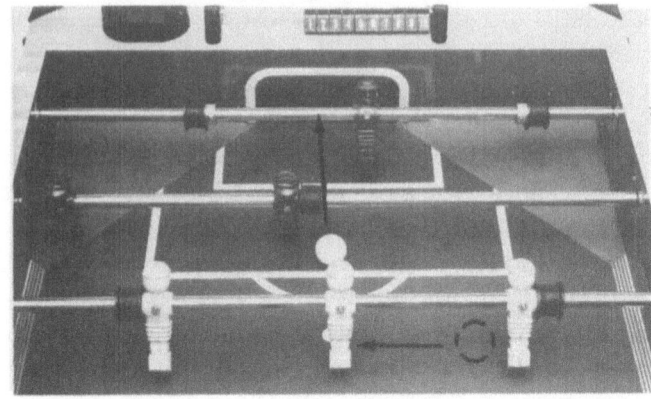

(13A) Dot shot

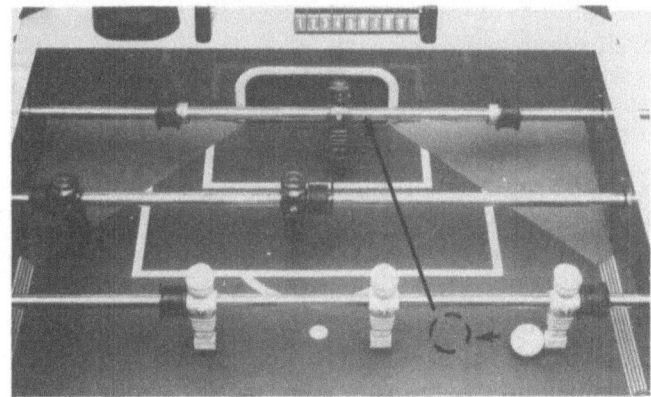

(13B) Dink

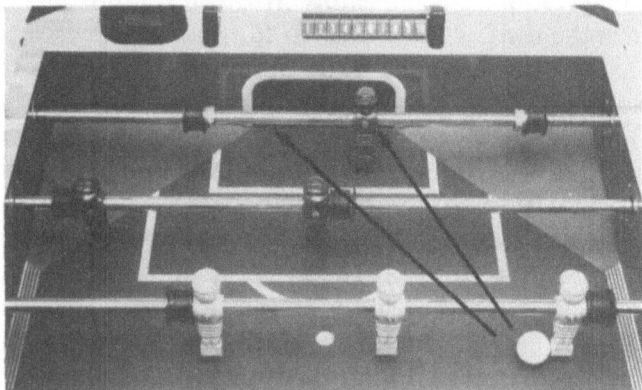

(13C) Angles

Figures 13A-13C: Pushkick offense options

fast enough that, if the goalie moves, he doesn't have time to jump back and block it, yet slow enough to give a goalie time to bail out of the hole.

Angle or Slice Shot. To round out your offense you'll need to learn both the behind, or short-hole, angle and the between, or middle, angle. The between angle is to be used on a reverse defense when the goalie is leaving a split between his or her men. Aim for the lip on the far side of the goal and chip about one-sixth of the ball. The middle angle should be shot at about medium speed. (See Figure 18A.)

Whether the goalie is using a crossover or a standard defense, the behind angle is an effective shot anytime the goalie leaves open the short hole. Aim for the short hole and chip about one-third of the ball. The behind angle must be shot a little harder than the between angle. (See Figure 13C.)

Pro Tip on the Pushkick—Ken Alwell

When I began playing foosball I thought all I needed was a fast, hard long shot. Quickly, I realized I was not going to score on a smart goalie unless I had a strong inside game to complement my long pushkick. From that point I worked to develop an array of options both to the short hole and to the middle hole.

The key to the inside game is to make the takeoff of each shot, whether it is a dink or an angle, the same speed as the takeoff you use for your long shot. This way the goalie cannot read your shot.

When reading the defense, try to pick the hole you want to shoot. Then wait out the goalie until the hole opens up, and execute the shot. Execution is the key to winning foosball! Regardless of whether you're scoring well, be sure to execute each shot on goal. This puts the pressure on the goalie.

More Pushkick Options

Once you have mastered the basic options, you may want to

try one of the following variations.

Hesitation or Doubletap Long. Softly tap the ball laterally about an inch and then shoot your long. The tap causes the goalie to hesitate or freeze and gives you time to shoot the ball around his or her defense.

Hard Push Shot. A good variation for shooting a middle or split. Push the ball the entire lateral distance of the no. 1 man and release it hard into the far end of the goal.

Middle Dink. Shoot this shot like the behind dink, but an inch farther and to the far side of the goal.

TECHNIQUE 2: THE PULL SHOT OFFENSE

The first step is to develop a long shot. Begin by setting the ball as in Figure 14A. The three-man rod should be positioned against the far wall with the ball directly underneath the rod and set up next to the middle man.

The main strength of a pull shot is the consistent ability to go longer than any other shot. If you intend to learn a pull shot, it's essential that you develop a quick, square long. By square long I mean you should learn to release your shot directly into the far corner of the goal. It should not angle out or cut back. Set the defense up in a crossover with the no. 1 man on the two-man rod, positioned just past the dot. This will make you shoot the ball squarely into the goal.

Now get into your stance. Check your grip. Pull the ball slowly but smoothly and try to concentrate on a hard release into the goal. For a good release, lay the ball back slightly. Your follow-through stroke should go back through the ball, causing your man to end up about an inch short of where the ball was released. (See Figure 14B.) This recoil will give you more power and also help you square the ball off. Continue practicing slow, hard, long shots until you develop confidence in your stroke. Depending upon the player and level of skill, this stage can vary from a few shots to a few days of hard practice. This is an important development stage in your game, since this is where

OFFENSIVE TECHNIQUES 59

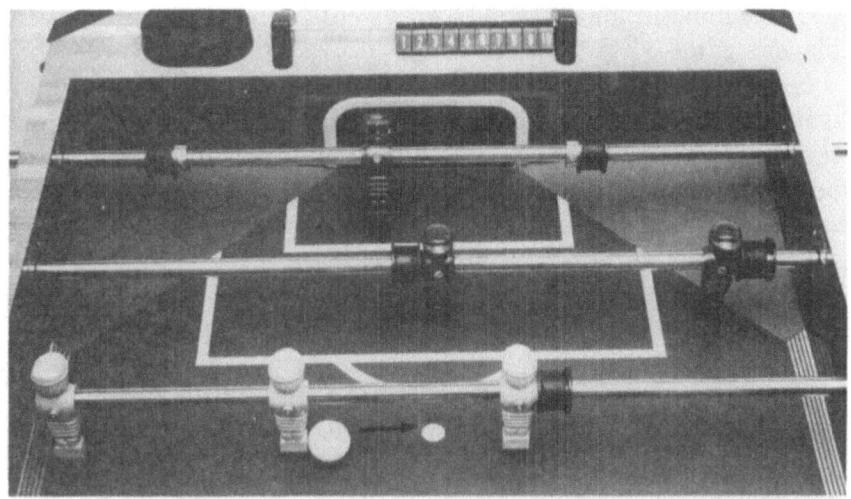

Figures 14A and 14B: Pull shot offense long shot

you develop the basic stroke, an essential fundamental in every player's game.

Once you have developed a consistent stroke, you should work to add speed to the shot. Do this a little at a time. Never sacrifice consistency for speed. With the proper practice you can be shooting quick, long pull shots in a few short weeks.

Pro Tip on the Pull Shot—Jim Wiswell

A good stance is an essential key to developing a consistent pull shot. Strive to develop a stance in which your body is well balanced. You should feel comfortable in the stance. Be sure to use the same stance each time you shoot in order to ensure consistency.

When I started playing, the first option I learned was a fast, hard, long pull shot. I feel a player must have a powerful long to be able to score on smart goalies. As your game progresses, you will need to learn the different options to the long. Be sure the takeoff on each shot looks the same, and you will not telegraph the shot to the goalie.

Pull Shot Options

Split or Middle Pull. The middle can be effective on both the crossover and the standard defenses. Anytime the goalie leaves a hole between his playing figures that is large enough for the ball, there is the possibility of scoring with a middle. Shoot a middle at the same speed as you would your long. Make it smooth and quick, not jerky. As you pull the ball laterally, concentrate on releasing the ball just past the first man in the defense. (See Figure 15A.) Don't worry about the second man in the defense, because he usually is in the process of moving out to cover the long hole. Therefore, if you pull the ball square just around the first defensive figure, you should always beat the second man. Always shoot the ball squarely or straight into the goal. Don't try to angle or cut the ball back, because a shot of this nature is usually inconsistent.

Straight In. A good straight shot is a must for a pull shot

OFFENSIVE TECHNIQUES 61

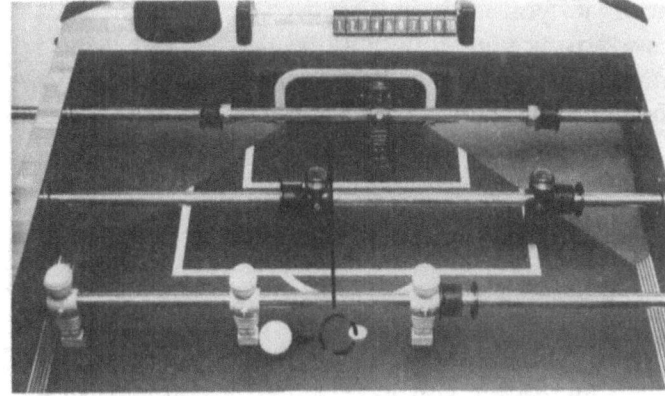

(15A) Split

(15B) Straight in

(15C) Angle

Figures 15A-15C: Pull shot offense options

offense. Without it you will not score on a smart goalie regardless of how strong your long may be.

To hit a straight, lift your man half an inch and stroke down and follow through the ball. (See Figure 15B.) Hit the ball medium hard, but don't try to kill it.

The straight shot can be used anytime a goalie is cheating and leaving open the short hole.

Other Options and Variations

Moving Straight. Sometimes you will find a goalie who will try to race your long. After you have scored a couple of longs, the goalie will get tense or jumpy. This is an excellent time to try a moving straight. Simply move the ball laterally about a quarter of an inch and then shoot the straight. This gives the goalie time to bail out of the hole, and you should score behind the defense.

Angle Between. The angle is a good shot to try when the goalie is in a crossover defense and leaves a hole between his or her men. From the set position chip about one-third of the ball at medium speed, causing the shot to go between the defense, ending up in the long hole. (See Figure 15C.)

TECHNIQUE 3: THE PULLKICK OFFENSE

A long pullkick can be effective using either the wrist or the palm roll release. Most pullkick shooters use the palm roll. However, a few pros have won tour events using a wrist pullkick. If you have decided to learn a pullkick, use whichever method is most comfortable and natural for you. The following fundamentals may be applied to both the palm roll and the wrist-style pullkick.

Begin by setting up the ball underneath the rod and even with the outside white line. (See Figure 16A.) For consistency, always try to start with the ball set up as closely to this position as possible. Next, arrange the defense in a crossover with the men positioned as in Figure 16A.

OFFENSIVE TECHNIQUES 63

Figures 16A-16B: A pullkick offense long shot

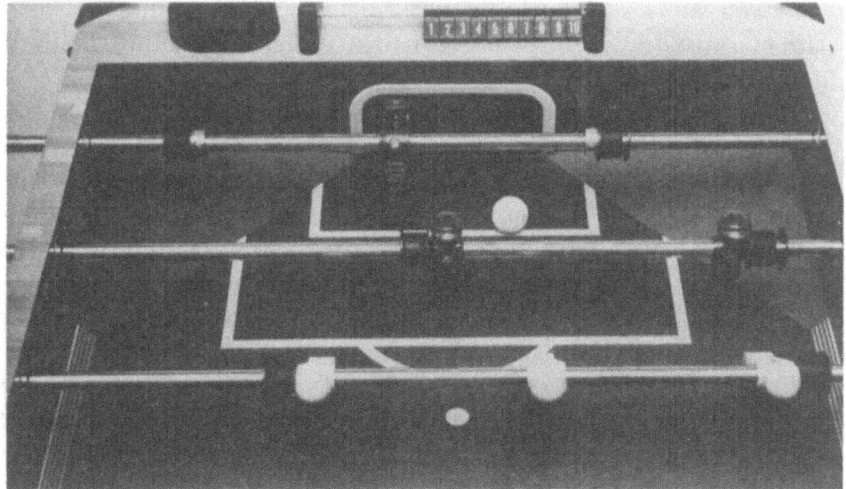

Now get into your stance. As you pull the ball toward you, lay it back slightly behind the rod in order to get a lot of power on the release (as in Figure 16B). Your first few shots should be slow and smooth. Concentrate on a good, crisp release. If you use the wrist style, your follow-through swing should go back through the ball, causing the ball to square off. Work at this speed until you develop confidence in your basic stroke. Once you feel confident, work to add more lateral speed to the shot.

Remember, this phase should be gradual. Don't sacrifice consistency for speed.

Pullkick Options

Dot Shot. The dot shot is executed with the same techniques as the long pullkick, only it is released over the dot. The correct time to use the dot shot is when the goalie is leaving a hole between the men in his or her defense. Effective on either a crossover or a standard defense, the dot shot should be performed smoothly and strongly, just as you would shoot the long shot. (See Figure 17A.)

Dink Shot. The pullkick dink is basically the same as the pushkick dink, except that it is shot from the opposite side. (See pushkick dink, page 55.) Pull the ball at a smooth pace with the no. 3 man, releasing it into the short hole with the same man. Try to make the takeoff look just like your long in order to make the goalie bail from the hole. Pullkick shooters who use the palm roll release should be sure to use a wrist release when doing a dink. (See Figure 17B.)

Angle. The same principles as described earlier for the angles off the pushkick set also apply to the pullkick. For the between angle, aim for the far lip and chip one-sixth of the ball at medium speed. To do the behind angle, chip one-third of the ball fairly hard and aim for the short hole. The pullkick angles can be effective with both wrist and roll releases. (See Figure 17C.)

OFFENSIVE TECHNIQUES 65

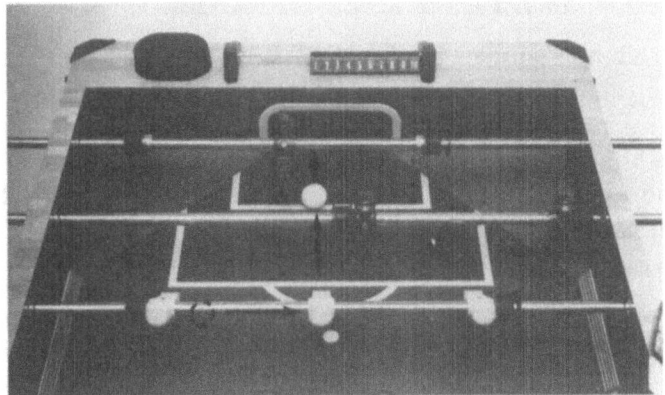

(17A)
Dot shot

(17B)
Dink shot

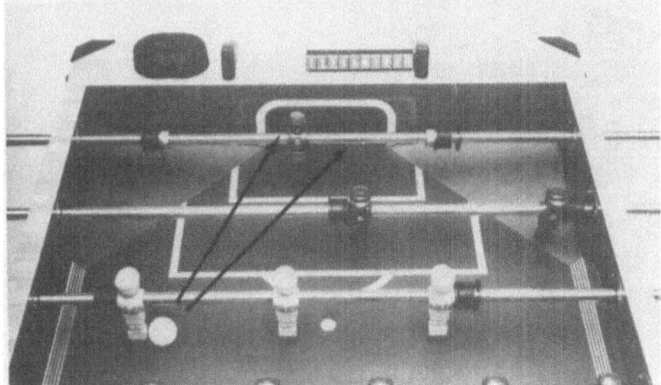

(17C)
Angles

Figures 17A-17C: Pullkick options

TECHNIQUE 4: THE PUSH SHOT OFFENSE

The push shot is similar to the pull shot, but it is shot from the opposite side of the goal. Begin with the ball positioned as in Figure 18A. The push is most effective when done using a wrist release. Use the same principles explained earlier for a pull shot. Practice shooting smooth longs until you develop a consistent stroke. Then work to add speed to the shot.

Options

For the push shot offense, your options include the straight

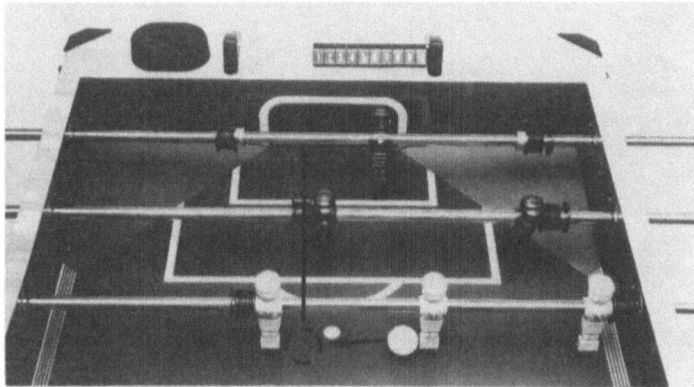

(18A)
Long hole

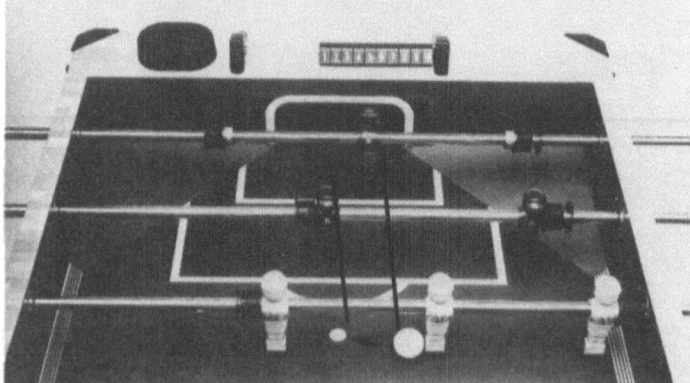

(18B)
Pushkick options

Figures 18A-18B: Push shot and options

in, short push between, angle between, and moving straight. Execute the options in the same manner as described earlier for the pull shot. (See Figure 18B.)

TECHNIQUE 5: BACKPIN SERIES

With the precision play tournament tables of today, ball control has become the name of the game. Increased ball control has caused an increased popularity in the backpin series. Many top pros use it as a secondary offense. Begin with the ball pinned between the center man and the playing surface, as in Figure 19. The ball should be set back far enough that you can

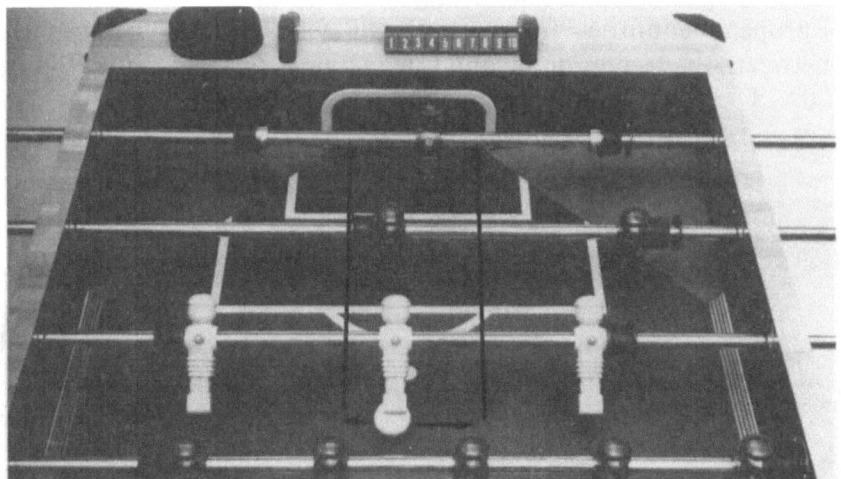

Figure 19: Backpin series

apply pressure without having the ball squirt out. There are two options to the long hole—either the outside or the inside corner of the goal. To go outside, push the pinned ball; to go inside, pull the pinned ball. As you move the ball laterally, lay the ball farther forward under the rod and use a wrist release into the goal.

Options

To go between or split a defense, simply move the ball in either direction about a half inch and reverse direction, shooting a short push or pull shot that splits the defense. You can also shoot a bank shot out of the backpin, to either the near or the far wall. Even pushkicks and pullkicks are effective. Simply maneuver the ball out of the pin and over to either the no. 1 or the no. 3 playing figure and come back with a push- or pullkick.

TECHNIQUE 6: FRONTPIN SERIES

When learned properly, the frontpin shot can be a very effective offense. Extremely popular among European players, the frontpin has dominated major championships in the various European countries for years. Begin with the ball frontpinned between the center man and the playing surface (as in Figure 20). The rod should be positioned against the far wall. The

Figure 20

best grip release for the frontpin is the palm roll. Using medium pressure on the ball, pull the ball toward you. Lay the ball back slightly behind the rod before releasing the ball into the long hole. This will give you more power on the release.

Options

Split. To shoot the split, simply shorten the normal frontpin stroke and release the ball between the playing figures of the defense.

Spin straight. To do the straight, spin the man one revolution counterclockwise, striking the ball into the goal. Legally, you have one revolution after striking the ball in which to catch the handle. You must be prepared to catch the handle immediately following the spin straight shot.

How to Develop Your Offense

It is very important that you properly develop your offense, the shot, and its options. In the early stages, your long shot will probably not be very fast. This is an important stage in the development of your game. Some rookies have a tendency to rush the normal skill progression by trying to shoot the long shot too fast. This can cause your shot to be jerky and inconsistent. Do not do this. Keep your shot smooth and increase the speed as you gain confidence, but not at the sacrifice of consistency. This is the stage of development in your game at which you must learn to understand goalie defenses and how to read which is the right hole to shoot for on a defense. Your long may not be quick enough to beat a goalie, but if it is consistent, he must move to block it. This leaves open one of your other options. If you have learned the options properly and can disguise all the takeoffs to look the same, you should be able to score by mixing up your shots and picking the right hole.

GOALIE POSITION

Technique 1: Shooting

The Bank Shot. A goalie who cannot do bank shots is like a football team which has no running game. Chances are that he just won't score. Developing a bank offense is very important to every player, goalie and forward alike. Every player needs to be able to clear the ball and score from the goalie position when playing a singles match.

Set Bank Shot. The first thing you must learn is proper ball positioning. Set the ball on the inside of the semicircle. Now position the ball directly behind your no. 1 man. Your man should be held directly straight up and down. The ball is now set in a position to do a bank shot to either wall. (This method of judging ball position will work anytime the ball is inside the semicircle. If you set the ball outside the semicircle, then it should be set up slightly farther forward to cut down on the angle of the shot.)

Now set your man on the side of the ball opposite the wall to which you are going to bank the ball. Example: If you're doing a far-wall bank, your man is on the near side of the ball. In order to get enough power on the ball, you should use a palm roll grip. Practically every player who shoots banks uses a palm roll because it is so much more powerful and consistent.

You are now ready to address the ball. Place your man directly on one-third of the ball. Begin your back swing and stroke through that third of the ball. If you swing straight through the ball with no lateral movement of the rod, then the ball should bank off the wall and into the goal. (See Figure 21.)

Don't be discouraged if your first bank shots lack crispness and power into the goal. Since you are probably trying bank shots for the first time, it is going to feel a little awkward at first. One way I've found to help develop a powerful swing is to take practice swings much like a golfer would do before driving

OFFENSIVE TECHNIQUES 71

Figure 21: Bank shot "set" position

the ball. Simply back your man an inch or so away from the ball and take a practice swing just as if you were going to strike the ball. Do this two or three times until you are confident with the stroke, then move up and address the ball.

If the ball is banking, but at too large or too small an angle, causing the shot to miss the goal, you may need to change the ball position slightly. If the ball is set slightly back, it will cause it to bank at a larger angle; if set too far forward, the shot will be at a smaller angle.

By experimenting with ball position, grip, and release, you should be able to develop a bank-type offense in less time than you might think. Most important, be patient and keep working at it—and it will come.

OPTIONS

If the opponent is covering your bank shots, there are many different options you can use. One is to push or pull the ball an inch or so and then bank it. This moves the ball out of the defense and opens up your chance of scoring.

You can also try a scoring option up the gut. This can be as simple as a straight shot at the goal or maybe a pull or push shot on goal. You might also want to throw in a couple of passes to your forward to offset your shooting. The main thing is to try to disguise your passes or shots so the opponent has little idea of what you will try next. This will keep the opponent off guard and help increase your shooting percentage. (Different types of passes are discussed later in this chapter.)

PIN BANK OFFENSE

Probably the most popular and widely used style of goalie offense is the backpin offense. It is easy to set up and requires only the ability to backpin the ball, yet it is very effective because there is no end to the possible options that can be used.

Begin by backpinning the ball on your inside playing figure of the two-man rod. From this position, roll the ball toward you an inch or so and try a far-wall bank. Don't roll the ball too fast at first; just use medium speed and concentrate on a good release on the bank shot. Practice this until you can consistently hit the far wall, then practice the same maneuver banking to the near wall.

Once you have mastered the backpin bank shots, there are many different types of banks to try. You can bank to the far or near wall using the outside man, using the inside man, or even passing the ball from one man to the other before banking it. You can roll the ball slow, fast, a short distance, or a long distance before shooting the bank. You can also roll the ball a distance, stop it, and then shoot the bank. This will sometimes cause the defense to overrun the ball, leaving either bank shot open.

Options

Gut Pin Straight. This is a simple option, yet very effective if executed properly. With the ball backpinned, advance it toward the center of the table as if you were going to do a bank shot. If the forward's three-man line is not covering the ball, shoot it straight and hard down the cut. This is an excellent way to clear the ball and leaves you the outside chance that it will score or bounce off the defending goalie to your forward's three-man row.

Other Options. There are many other up-the-gut options to the pin bank series. You can do push or pull shots, pushkicks, pullkicks, and even reverses. You can also throw in a few different types of passes. Remember to try to disguise your offense so the different shots and passes catch your opponent off guard.

Pro Tip on Goalie Offense—Doug Furry

To score well from the goalie position requires much versatility. The player should be able to score from any position on the table with a variety of shots. It requires not only skill but plenty of practice to master the different shots and options you'll need as a goalie.

When I am competing, I prefer to keep the ball moving continuously in a fluid motion from one playing figure to another. As I move the ball, I am constantly looking for a hole to open up in the defense. When I spot a hole, whether it is a straight or a bank, I shoot it immediately and hopefully score.

Sometimes if the opponent is playing a fast pace or aggressive defense, I will stop the ball, set it up for a pull shot or a push shot, and concentrate on clearing the ball to the other end of the table. This way I might score and many times the ball will bounce off the opposite goalie's defense and my forward will end up with the ball.

Technique 2: Wrist Shots

Set pull shots, pullkicks, push shots, and pushkicks can all be effective from the goalie position. They provide an excellent way to clear the ball past the forward and have a reasonably good chance of scoring. However, many teams have sophisticated zones for these set shots, and, in order to score on a zone, you'll need a couple of good options.

For example, if you like to shoot a pullkick from the goalie you might throw in a pullkick bank to either wall. Or, if you like to use a push shot, you might develop a strong push bank to one wall or the other as an option. If you use your imagination, there is no limit to the possible combinations and variations you can use in a goalie offense. Unlike the forward position, in which a player needs one strong shot with a few good options in order to win, a goalie has the versatility to use many different shots, even during tournament competition.

Technique 3: Passing

Passing can be an important part of a goalie's offense, especially in doubles play. Most professional goalies pass at least 10 to 15 percent of the time, and some as often as 30 to 40 percent. The object in passing is to get the ball to your forward so he or she can score. Obviously, there are right and wrong times to attempt passes. The following are a few hypothetical situations:

Good times to pass:

1. When your forward is hot. If you complete a pass, it's almost as good as scoring.
2. When you are having problems clearing the ball on your shots. You might complete a pass, and the worst thing that can happen is that you won't clear the pass either!
3. When your forward is being out-fived on the five-man. If your forward is just not getting enough of his passes through, you should try to get the ball to him so he won't lose his stroke or his confidence.

Bad times to pass:

1. When you're playing a forward who seems to key or look for passes, making a pass difficult to complete.
2. When your forward is getting shut out or blocked by the goalie. This is when you should try to score!

OFFENSIVE TECHNIQUES 75

Figure 22: Pull pass

There are many different types of passes. Most passes work best when done through either lane closest to the wall to either outside man on the three-man line. The reason for this is that when you try a pass, the defending forward's natural tendency is to bail to the wall with the three- and five-man lines, leaving that lane wide open.

PULL PASS

This pass, popularized by Minnesota goalies, is simple to do and can be very effective. With the ball set inside the semicircle, pull the ball about two inches and release it at an angle down the lane. (See Figure 22.) This pass should be made quickly but smoothly at about three-quarters of the normal speed. Note: Be sure that your forward is expecting the pass. Signal him by tapping the forward's foot, or doing something along that line so he knows the pass is coming, but the opponents don't.

Figure 23: Goalie pass

GOALIE PASS

This pass is popular among goalies who use a pin bank type of offense. Begin with the ball backpinned on the far man of your two-man rod. Now pull the ball toward you at about medium speed and have your goalie positioned on the inside corner of the goal. Using the far man, pass the ball back to the goalie man, who in turn passes the ball downfield through the lane to the forward. (See Figure 23.) The lateral momentum of the ball should cause it to angle naturally just enough to go through the lane.

How to Develop Your Goalie Offense

As I have mentioned, the number of shots or passes that a goalie can use is endless. However, this does not mean that you set out to develop a reckless, inconsistent array of different shots and passes. The most important factor in a shot or pass is clearing the ball—getting the ball past your opponent's three- and five-man lines. This is your first offensive job as a goalie. If, by clearing the ball ten times in a game, you happen to score one or two points, that's great. However, if you are too worried about scoring each time you touch the ball, causing you to try fancy or somewhat reckless shots, you may end up scoring more points but also getting stuffed and turning the ball over twice, which will end up costing you or your team the game.

In short, you should develop your offense at the goalie position in ways similar to those with which a forward would develop an offense. For each of your strong shots you need a couple of good options and at least one pass, all of which should begin in the same position, off the same set and look somewhat similar. Therefore, the opponent is never sure which option you will use next. Experiment with new shots or passes anytime you're playing just for fun; if a shot or pass shows potential, then practice it, get it down, and add it to your offense. Thus, when you're playing a serious game or match, your offense should consist mainly of test-proven shots and passes that you can execute consistently and with complete confidence.

7
Defensive Techniques

Aggressive, get-down defense can mean the difference between winning and losing. Beginning players sometimes tend to put too much emphasis on the offensive part of the game, while neglecting the defensive aspects. Competitive foosball is a closely balanced combination of offense and defense, and many times a game, a match, or even a tournament can be decided by one blocked pass or shot. Every player, whether forward or goalie, should develop a solid understanding of defensive strategy. Whether you're a goalie facing a pull shot or a forward going up against a precision five-man, be prepared not only with a confident defensive set, but also with two or three backup sets in case your usual defense isn't working. By developing depth in your defensive game, you can avoid some of the frustrations many players experience when they just can't seem to stop any shot.

DEFENSIVE TECHNIQUES 79

(24A)

(24B)

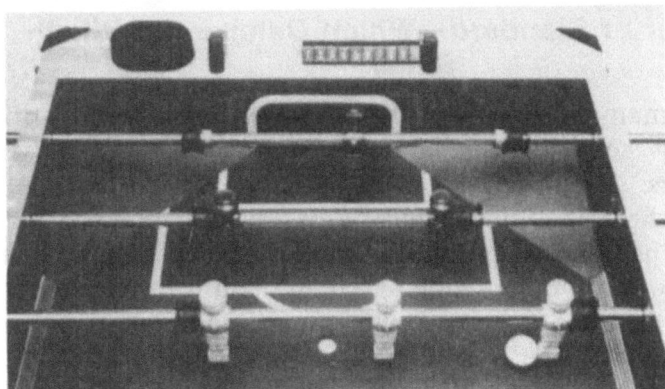

(24C)

Figures 24A-24C: Standard defenses

GOALIE POSITION

Technique 1: Standard Defense

The two basic defenses at the goalie position—the standard defense and the crossover defense—use two playing figures: the goalie on the one-man rod, and one of the two playing figures on the two-man rod. The standard defense uses the goalie to cover the outside portion of the goal, and the playing figure on the two-man rod closest to the place where the shot is set to cover the inside portion of the goal. (See Figures 24.) In other words, while using the standard defense, the location of the goalie playing figure remains between the two playing figures on the two-man rod, which is the standard position for these rods when not in play.

Technique 2: Crossover Defense

The crossover defense, or reverse defense, uses the goalie playing figure to cover the inside portion of the goal. The playing figure on the two-man rod nearest to the place where the ball is set is used to cover the outside portion of the goal. This is done by reversing the standard position of the playing figures involved. (See Figures 25A, 25B, and 25C.)

Crossover or Standard—Which Defense for Which Shot?

There are many reasons why the crossover defense will work better against some players, and the standard defense better against others. A crossover defense cuts down the angle of scoring into the goal. For example, a person who shoots a pull shot that, rather than squaring off, angles into the long hole, is more likely to score on a standard defense than on a crossover. However, if the shooter has a long, square pull shot, you are probably better off using a standard defense.

Different defenses have different psychological effects on shooters. Many pull shot shooters feel very confident about

DEFENSIVE TECHNIQUES 81

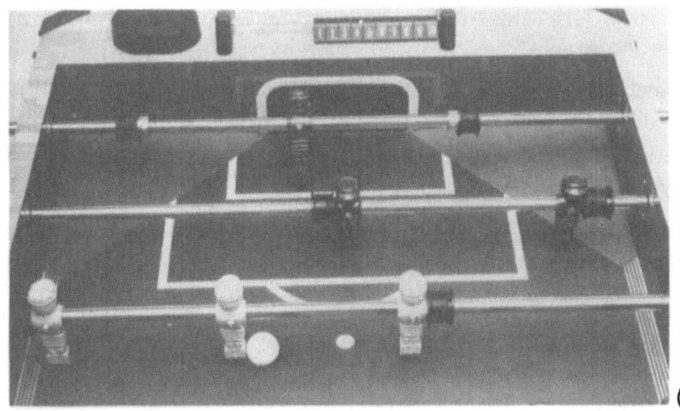
(25A)

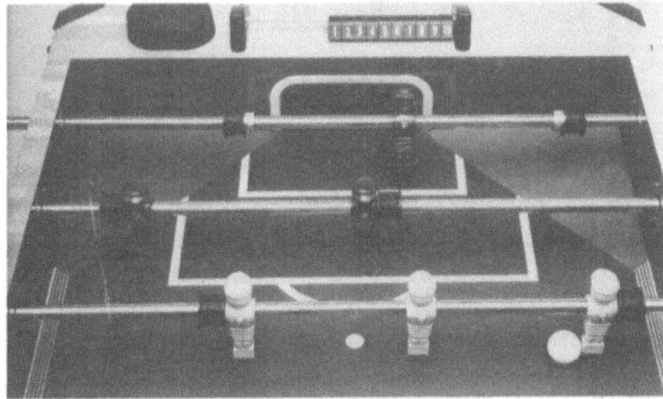
(25B)

(25C)

Figures 25A-25C: Crossover defenses

scoring their long shot against a crossover—that lead playing figure on the two-man gives them a target to shoot around. It is purely psychological, but they shoot more confidently in that situation. A shooter suddenly facing a defense he has had trouble with before will most likely shoot with less confidence.

Most important, however, is your feel for the defense. Are you more comfortable and confident using a crossover or a standard? Chances are greater that you will be scored on if you are uncomfortable with or uncertain of your defense. You must weigh all the factors and use the defense that works best for you.

Technique 3: The Race

Most players learning the goalie position will begin by using some type of still race defense. This means that they sit still in front of the ball and, as their opponent moves the ball, they move with the opponent and try to race him or her to the open hole. The race forces your opponent to go for the long hole, and to do it fast enough to beat you there. As simple as it may seem, the race defense is one of the most difficult defenses to master and execute properly. You need quick reflexes and the ability to analyze your opponent's timing and shooting habits.

The first thing I do when racing someone is to analyze his or her shot. Exactly how does he or she shoot each option? Is the opponent's dink or moving straight done with the same takeoff speed as his or her long? Concentration is of the utmost importance. The first few shots of the game should determine whether or not a race will be a successful defense in this case. Don't start the game by racing at full speed, but rather at about three-quarter speed, watching out for the dink or moving straight. This way, you have the inside and short hole covered, and you still have a chance to race and block your opponent if he shoots long. It's very important that you make a mental record of the first few shots. Remember exactly how each one looked whether you blocked it or not.

Once you have a good idea of what your opponent's offense looks like, test it with a full race. To do this, stare at the ball and concentrate on what the opponent's dink (or moving straight, if you're playing a pull or push shot shooter) looks like.

Your natural reaction is to jump long when the ball moves. Because of this, as soon as the ball moves, you must decide whether or not the opponent has tried a dink. If so, you must stop yourself in time to block that shot. If your opponent tries a long, go with your instinct and race long.

Remember, the race is a tough defense to master. It is not for everyone. The best time to try it is against an opponent who has a slow shot or some other weakness that allows you to distinguish among the options in his offense.

Pro Tip on Defense—Brent Bednar

I have always felt that the race defense is the best overall defense. It forces the opponent to shoot a well-executed fast shot in order to score.

However, to use a race requires not only quick reflexes but good anticipation. When racing from a still position, I pick out a speck on the ball, concentrate on that speck, and the instant it moves I make the decision either to race long or to freeze for the dink. The takeoff of the shooter is the key to that decision. You can usually notice a difference between the takeoff of a long and that of a dink.

Sometimes I will try to anticipate the shot. To be able to do this, you must get into the player's head and try to anticipate what he or she is thinking. Just when you feel that the person is about to shoot, move your defense out into the long hole. If you anticipate correctly, the opponent will shoot right into your defense. Otherwise, you should quickly move your men back into the short hole.

Technique 4: The Louisiana Shuffle

At the 1974 $50,000 Denver tournament, a team from Louisiana placed third in doubles. Excellent defensive play by the goalie was a big factor in their success, and his style of defense has come to be known as the Louisiana Shuffle.

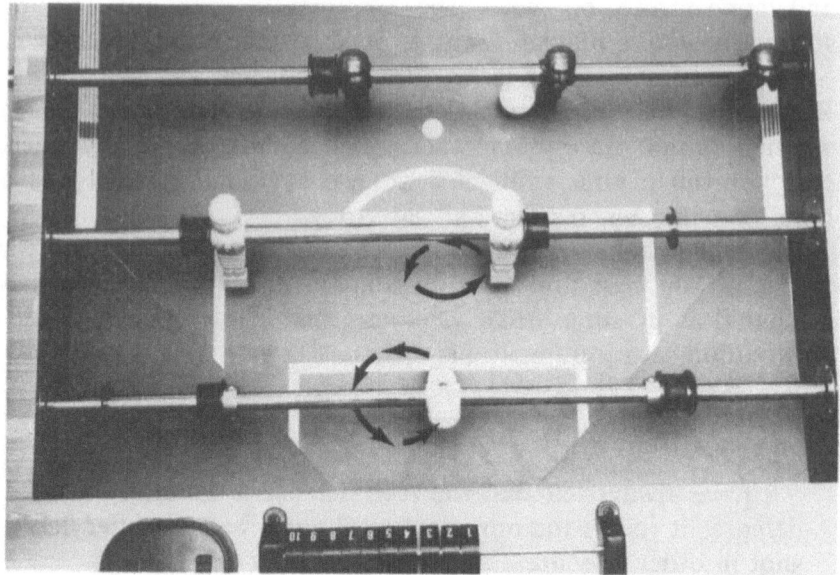

Figure 26: Moving defense

The theory behind the Louisiana Shuffle is that moving the feet of the playing figures in quick circular motions covers more of the goal area and therefore makes it more difficult to score—like trying to throw a baseball through the propeller of an airplane.

Anyone can use the Louisiana Shuffle. With a little practice, it is an excellent defense, especially for beginners. Start out in a standard or a crossover, whichever you like. When the forward is ready to shoot, begin moving your men in fast circles about an inch in diameter. (See Figure 26.) To vary the defense, you can try faster or slower circles, larger or smaller circles, clockwise or counterclockwise circles. Be careful that you do not try to cover too large an area with your circles, or you will find yourself using a defense that is everywhere, but nowhere!

Technique 5: Random Defense

Sometimes you will face a player whose shot seems to have no real weakness. He or she shoots a fast long and has good inside and middle options. This is when many goalies will try a random defense.

The idea is to switch from one defense to another—from a standard to a crossover, for example—and to constantly change the holes being covered. For instance, against a pull shot you might start out in a standard, leaving open the long hole, then switch to a crossover, leaving the middle hole. Then, just as the shooter is about to try the middle, switch back to a standard, but this time, instead of leaving the long hole open, leave the straight.

Sound confusing? It should. The object is to confuse the shooter by randomly leaving different holes open. It's a good idea to try to switch just before the player shoots. This way he can't possibly know which hole will be open, and scoring becomes a cat-and-mouse guessing game.

Be careful that your random defense does not develop a predictable pattern and timing. What makes this defense effective is its unpredictable nature.

Developing Defense at the Goalie Position

In order to develop depth in your defense against various shots, you need to be innovative. Watch other goalies and learn from their techniques. Don't hesitate to copy a defense you've seen someone else use successfully, even if it means changing it slightly to fit your style. There are thousands of strategic combinations that can be used to defend the goal. Fast motions, slow motions, still defenses, switching, circular motions, jabbing, flicking, racing, anticipating, baiting—these are just a few variations that can be tried. Don't be afraid to experiment. If you are getting drilled, try something else. If that doesn't work, try something else! The worst that can happen is that you will keep getting scored on. It is likely, however, that if you keep trying, some defense is bound to work.

What else can you do to be a good defensive goalie? Stay alert! Your main function at the goalie position is to keep the ball from scoring in your goal. You must be ready for any situation that might arise. The fact that the other forward has the ball on his or her five-man line is no reason for you to relax. That forward may pass the ball to his or her three-man every time right up to game point, and then, just when you're lulled into thinking the forward is going to pass, Wham! The player scores a five-man shot and the game is over. You should always be ready for a five-man shot, or ready to catch and control the ball if the other forward misses the pass or if it is deflected by your forward. Remember, it is the little things a player does that can mean the difference between winning and losing. Never relax and let your mind wander when your forward is getting ready to shoot—his shot could hit the wall and come right back at you to score for the other team.

Desire, concentration, and alertness—that's what it all comes down to. If you really desire to win, then you will concentrate and be prepared at all times so that you can give your best effort to prevent your opponent from scoring.

FORWARD POSITION

Technique 1: Five-Man Defense

At the tournament level, five-man defense can be the most important part of the defensive game. Regardless of how powerful a shot your opponent may have, he or she cannot score without first getting the ball. Since the passing series of most players are executed in a small area (usually the sidewall and the playing area one to two inches in front of it), you must try to defend against those passes with only one playing figure. This means moving your five-man row in many different patterns at varying speeds in order to cover that area. Keep alert and always watch for a weakness or other tendency your opponent may have. For example, a player may tend to do most of his or her passes to the wall. If so, camp your defense on the wall and race to cover any passes that player tries off the wall. Other players prefer to pass in the lane off the wall. If so, take that away from them and race to the wall.

Be sure to check and see where the player sets the three-man line before passing. Some players give away the pass by where they position their three-man to catch it.

If you seem to be bailing for each and every fake, try to concentrate more on your defense and your men rather than staring directly at the ball. This way you will not overreact if the player tries a fake, yet you know which hole you are leaving open so that you can react and try to stop the pass.

To sum up five-man defense, I want to point out that you should not feel too frustrated if a player completes his or her passes through your defense. You have only one man to cover the two main passing lanes. The odds are in his or her favor, so stay alert, watch for key weak points in the opponent, and play very persistent, aggressive defense on every play. There is no room for frustration!

Technique 2: The Fork Defense

A bank shot from the opposing goalie is often difficult to defend against for an inexperienced player. I can still remember the first time I ever played a goalie who used a bank shot offense. The match was over before I knew what had happened.

The first thing you should be aware of is that the main responsibility for blocking goalie bank shots belongs to the forward. Once a bank gets past the forward's three-man and five-man lines, its chances of scoring are very high. In order to stop bank shots, the forward needs to use a fork defense. This means that the three-man row is positioned in a way that blocks the angles to the wall. To do this, tilt the three-man row forward and keep the ball directly centered between two of the playing figures at all times. As you can see in Figure 27, this will cut off the angle at which both the inside and the outside banks are shot. While it sounds simple, it will take some practice to get used to it. Many goalies move the ball all around before shooting it, and you must learn to follow their every movement in order to keep the shots covered. You are right if you're thinking that the fork defense leaves the straight shots open.

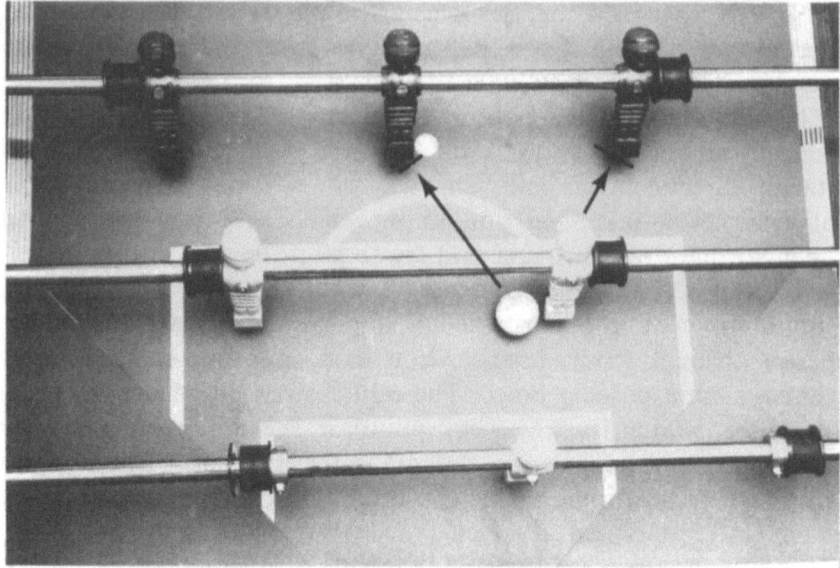

Figure 27: Bank defense "fork defense"

This is where a team zone comes in. While the forward covers the banks, the goalie blocks the straights.

Technique 3: The Zone Defense

Coordination of the goalie and forward rods can zone out or prevent the opponent from scoring a high percentage of shots from the goalie position.

The object of the zone defense is to position the three-man and five-man rods in such a way that the only channels open to the opponent are those being covered at the other end by your goalie. (See Figure 28.)

In the most commonly used zone defense, the forward blocks the banks by using a fork defense, while the goalie covers the straights. If the bank goes past the forward's three-man, he or she should try to catch it with the five-man—most banks hit the wall at or near the five-man row. A goalie who sees a bank shot

DEFENSIVE TECHNIQUES 89

Figure 28: Zone defense

coming that the forward has missed should naturally react by trying to block the shot. The fact that the banks are the forward's responsibility does not mean that the goalie should make no effort to help out. It does take a great deal of experience at the goalie position to be able to read the angle of a bank and move to the correct position to block that shot, but it can be done. A good team defense does not develop out of placing blame on your partner for a shot missed. Awareness of responsibilities is necessary, but a genuine team effort by both players is the key to a strong defensive game.

8
Valuable Tips for the Advanced Player

Competitive foosball is a highly complicated sport. Many players today possess both the desire and the ability to win on any given day, but it is often the little things a player overlooks that can mean the difference between winning and losing. As you read this chapter, I hope you will not only learn a tip or two that may improve your game, but also come to realize the amount of precision involved in the tournament style of play. On each play you must try to use your best percentage pass or shot. Competitive foosball is like a game of chess: one mistake can be all it will take to put you in checkmate.

GOALIE PLAY

Offensive Tip

One of the biggest mistakes many goalies make is getting too involved in watching the defense while trying to shoot. One method to use is to decide which shot to try, block out the defense, and keep your eyes on the ball. Many times a forward will switch defenses to confuse you. Don't let this bother or distract you. Try to choose the right shot and then concentrate 100 percent on proper execution.

Defensive Tip for Blocking Forwards

Most goalies react well as long as the defense they are using is working to some degree. The difference between a mediocre goalie and a strong goalie is the ability to change defenses intelligently when he or she is getting scored on, until something finally works. Once a goalie starts getting drilled, he or she usually resorts to some type of radical defense, which usually also fails. Many times the reason for this is simply that the player is too frustrated to think calmly.

Before every major tournament I sit down and make up a defensive card. On this card I list a number of good defenses that I have used successfully against certain shots in the past. For instance, I might list four pushkick defenses, five pullkick, and five pull shot defenses. This way, in the middle of a match, if the defense I'm using starts getting scored on, I simply take a time-out, look at my defensive card, and immediately call to mind a defense to use—not some radical, desperation move, but a defense I have used before and in which I have confidence.

Pro Tip on Goalie Defense—Mike Bowers

The key to consistent goalie defense is the ability to remain calm, especially if you are getting scored on. Don't panic! Remain calm and analyze the situation. Be sure to give a defense at least a game to work before you switch. After a game or so, if a defense is still not working, then don't be afraid to switch to another type of defense. Stay relaxed, keep your composure, and make sure you execute the new defense correctly.

Defensive Tips against Opposing Goalie Shots

Many goalies sometimes try to shoot the ball hard and

straight up the gut, hoping that the ball will bounce off the opponent's front man and be picked up by their forward. For practical purposes this is just the same as if that goalie completed a beautiful pull pass to his forward. A smart goalie will not allow the opposing goalie to do this. There are a couple of things you can do in order to prevent this. I have found that continually flicking your leading defensive man when the opposing goalie is shooting works best. This flick motion will usually either shoot the ball back toward the other end or cause it to fly off your man to either side. It should keep the ball from bouncing off your man to the opposing forward.

Passing

Almost all goalies pass to their forwards at least occasionally. The problem with many goalies is that they take it for granted that their forward knows which pass is coming and when. I recommend that you always signal your forward before you pass. Some goalies will tap their forward on the foot. This is okay, but the forward still isn't sure which pass you will try. Also, there is the chance that the other team will pick up your signal. If you have a steady partner, work out a simple method of signaling. It could be the number of times you bounce the ball off the wall, fake, or even pin the ball in certain positions. You'll find that, if your forward knows which pass is coming and when, your percentage of passes completed will begin to increase.

FORWARD POSITION

Reading a Defense

Many players possess a strong shot but have difficulty choosing the correct hole in the defense. Random and fast-switching defenses are often confusing. You must be decisive and time the holes as they open and close. Next time you are having trouble reading a certain defense, try one of the following systems.

PERCENTAGE READ

Instead of looking at the entire defense and trying to pick a hole, first decide which hole you want to shoot. For example, let's say you decide to shoot long. You should also have a secondary shot in mind. Let's say a straight. Okay, you get set—you are ready to shoot. You look for the long hole. If it's open, you shoot it and score. But if it's not, you immediately shoot the straight. This way, if one man is covering the long, or whichever hole you have chosen to shoot, shooting the secondary shot immediately gives you a 50/50 chance of scoring.

COUNT SYSTEM

The count system is good to use whenever you are totally confused by the defense. Okay, you are set and ready to shoot. With the count system, you don't even look at the defense. Concentrate on the ball and your execution. First, decide which hole you are going to shoot and on what count; for example, a long on a five-count. Count to five to yourself and then shoot long.

By varying the count and shots at random, you can often score better than by trying to observe the defense. Good goalies spend many practice hours working up defenses with moves designed to bait or trick you into shooting into the wrong hole. By using a count system and not watching the goalie's moves, you will shoot the shot you want and force the goalie to block you.

Pro Tip on Passing for Five-Man Offense—Tom Spear

Many players, even some pros, don't take their time on the five-man. You have a full ten seconds, and I try to use that to my advantage on each and every pass.

Move the ball around and play with it a little before attempting the pass. This forces your opponents always to be ready on defense. By the end of the match you may even find the opponent has tired and his defense has slowed somewhat.

Sometimes I like to set up my opponent. I try to make it look obvious that I am going to try a certain pass and then instead I do just the opposite.

CONDITIONING AND PREPARATION FOR TOURNAMENT PLAY

Foosball may not seem to be a physically demanding sport; however, tournament play often requires three or sometimes four days of hard aggressive play. In order to maintain a sharp, competitive edge throughout an entire tournament, a player must possess a high level of mental and physical stamina. This is evident from the excellent physical characteristics of many of the top foosball champions of both past and present. Most professional foosers are in top shape and maintain themselves by working out, running, or by some other type of regular exercise.

While professionals agree with the statement that a player must be in good condition to endure the physical strain of tournament play, the most important reason for being in top condition is the mental effect it can have on a player. Foosball is a head game, and winning tournaments requires an enormous amount of self-control and mental endurance. As a tournament reaches its final day, many players find themselves weak or tired, often during the middle of a match. If your body tires easily, then your concentration and level of intensity will soon follow suit. To adhere to a regular exercise program takes will power and much self-control, but if your goal is to be a winner, I can't think of two more important traits to develop.

Most professional players begin preparation for a big tournament at least one month before the event. A daily schedule should be set up that includes some type of exercise to build up your body's stamina. Running is an excellent endurance builder and also provides a convenient time to concentrate mentally on winning. Swimming, racquetball, and tennis are also excellent conditioning exercises. Some players like to lift weights to build their strength. This is okay, but don't overdo it. Work out with light to medium weights and make sure your last workout is at least three full days before the tournament. This is to make sure you won't be too tight or too sore to give your best possible performance.

Practice Routine

It's important that you create and adhere to a consistent practice schedule prior to an important tournament. Depending on the individual and the importance of the tournament, this may cover a few days or a few months of time. Put together a set routine that consists of at least five to ten repetitions of each shot and option in your offense. Set aside a time at which to go through this routine at least once every day. This will give you complete confidence in the execution of your game.

As for reading of defenses, defensive play, and all-around practice, you should try to put in as much play against local competition as possible. When you go out and play, try to get as much out of each session as you can. Play as if you were exposed to actual tournament conditions. Try to pinpoint any weaknesses in your game so you can work to improve these points prior to the upcoming tournament.

It takes self-discipline to stick to a practice schedule. Make a commitment to yourself, stand by it, and it will pay off in the end.

Doubles Play

While some players prefer to excel in singles, many regard doubles as the more challenging game. Doubles play presents the challenge of coordinated teamwork, the necessity for precise ball control, and the exhilarating feeling of victory, which can be most fulfilling when shared with a partner.

The strength of a winning doubles team almost always lies in the ability of the two players to use teamwork and strategy in order to control the tempo of play during the game and the match. In other words, two superior singles players do not necessarily make a good doubles team. You must play with a partner who will complement your game or style of play, and much time should be spent in developing team strategy, game plans, and a general knowledge of each other's strengths and weaknesses.

Some professional players successfully team together in doubles, yet they live a great distance apart and are unable to practice together on a regular basis. This is fine if you've been playing for many years and have the ability to meet your partner at a tournament, practice together for a few hours, and gain the confidence required to win tournaments. However, this is rarely the case with a novice or less experienced player. Ideally the beginning player should recruit a partner who lives in the same city or general vicinity. This doesn't necessarily mean you should seek out the best player in your area. Rather, look for a player who you feel has the potential to be a winner. The person should be dedicated and willing to spend the practice hours essential to developing a good team effort. By teaming up with a local player, you can practice many more hours. Time is needed to develop ball control and team strategy. Most important, you have the opportunity to test your skills and strategies against local competition on a regular basis. The experience you and your partner receive through play against the local competition will make you more confident when you compete in professional events.

Learn the Rules

I can't stress enough the importance of knowing and understanding the rules before you enter a tournament. The rules are constantly being upgraded and revised, so you need to be sure you have the latest copy of the official WTSA rules. When you get to the tournament, check with the head official to make sure you are acquainted with any last-minute changes or revisions that may have been made.

Pressure and the Mental Game

Winning foosball definitely depends more on mental factors than on physical factors. Many players possess the skill required, but only a few manage to harness the secret to a positive mental attitude.

First of all, many beginning players—sometimes even pros—don't seem to take tournaments seriously. Oh, sure, it looks as if they are getting down during the match, but between matches you can find them cruising the room, socializing among friends. The time between matches is the most important of all. You must stay warmed up and be psychologically ready for each match. If your match is not called immediately, then you should shoot a rack or two of practice shots every ten minutes.

Try to find out who your next opponent is going to be and scout out his or her strengths and weaknesses. If you're a goalie and you're going to be playing a pull shooter, then find someone who has a good pull shot and have him or her shoot a few racks against you to warm up your defense. If you're a forward, you might try to find someone who passes in a similar fashion to your next opponent so you can warm up your five-man defense. Most important of all, you must keep up your mental attitude and level of concentration between each and every match.

During a game, the key to winning is concentration. You must be able to concentrate and perform your best 100 percent of the time. This is what distinguishes the winner from the loser. If you watch the top professionals, you will see that they rarely let anything affect or disturb them during the play of the game. Most pros develop some habit to help increase their concentration and get them through pressure situations. Some players chew gum, some fidget or follow finicky habits, and some even talk to themselves during play to calm themselves and relax the tension and pressure of the situation. Taking a deep breath before an important pass or shot always seems to help relieve some of the tension.

Try to prevent your mind from wandering beyond the ball that is in play. Becoming distracted by other matters is the primary reason a player becomes nervous or feels pressured. For example, the score in a game should never affect you. Don't try to win games; instead, score points. The best come-from-behind players are those who take one point at a time rather than worrying about the score. Before they know it, they are back in the game and the match. Steve Simon, one of the best comeback and pressure players, says that he believes foosball momentum can easily change during a game or even a match. If his opponent scores two or three consecutive points, Steve believes the odds are that if he stays "down" and concentrates 100 percent, it will be his turn to score the next few points and get back into the game. Whether this is right or wrong, Steve has managed to come up with a way to make himself play harder and more confidently when the chips are down. Many players could learn a lesson from this, since a lot of foosers tend to give up when they find themselves behind 3-0 or 4-1 in a game.

Pro Tip on the Mental Aspect of the Game— Steve Simon

If a player is completely confident in his or her ability at the table, then pressure shouldn't hurt the player. A pressure situation causes a person's adrenalin to rise. It's a well-known fact that a person's reaction to adrenalin is a fight-or-flight type of response.

Confident players will channel the energy created by the pressure into a positive direction, which helps them rise to the occasion. On the other hand, less confident players often let the energy channel in a negative direction, which causes them to perform poorly.

As long as you are completely confident in both your offense and your defense, you are going to react positively to pressure situations.

Just as important as not thinking ahead is not worrying about things that have already happened. Many players are upset when the opponent scores a couple of sloppy points. All this does is hurt your concentration. You have no power to change what has already happened. Just as surely as football players will fumble and baseball players will drop balls, foosball players are going to score occasional lucky or accidental shots. Learn to accept each point as just another point and go on to the next ball, whether the shot was accidental, lucky, or picture perfect. They all count one point!

Another mistake players make is to get too mad or frustrated when they or their partners miss a shot or get scored on. Again, this just takes your concentration away from the ball in play and, if you are yelling at your partner, it will also ruin his concentration. The best thing you can do if your partner is having problems is not to worry about him and try to play your very best in your position.

The secret to a positive mental attitude and strong concentration level is locked up in every player's mind. The key which any player may use to unlock this is self-control. How can you expect to control your opponent if you can't even control your own emotions? By developing self-control you can learn to ignore anything that might distract or alarm the average player, and to play your best when you're behind or in clutch situations. This edge will make the difference between winning points, games, matches, and tournaments.

9
Trick Shots

Every foosball player would like to be able to razzle dazzle or amaze his or her friends with fancy ball control and trick shots. In this chapter, you will find a few of the fancy shots and maneuvers I have invented or learned in my years as a fooser. With practice, most of these shots can be developed with some degree of consistency. For a beginner, a few of the moves may seem a bit difficult; however, don't be discouraged. Remember, it has taken the best players in the world years even to think of some of the trick shots in this chapter!

FORWARD POSITION

Bank Shots

Probably the most amazing shot to a crowd of bar players is a bank shot from the three-man rod. Ironically, the three-man bank is really not so difficult to learn.

Begin by backpinning the ball with the middle man. The middle man is best to use because it is easier to bank to both

TRICK SHOTS 101

Figure 29: Forward bank shot

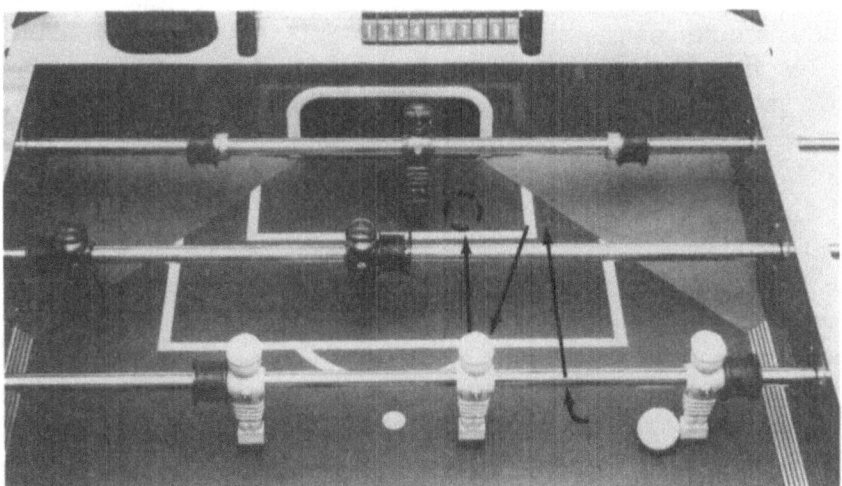

Figure 30: Rebound smash

walls. Now, with the ball securely pinned, move your man slightly to the side of the ball opposite the wall to which you wish to bank. Your man should now be on about a third of the ball (as in Figure 29). Now, using either the wrist or the palm roll technique, crank down on the one-third area of the ball. The ball should bank off the wall into the goal. You may need to adjust the position of the ball if the bank is not on goal.

The Rebound Smash

This shot is fairly easy to learn, yet almost unbelievable when seen the first time. When I score this shot, the reaction of most players is to ask me whether it was just lucky or a planned shot!

Set up the ball on your inside man on the three-man rod as if you were about to do a pushkick. Now, push the ball about an inch and a half and release it, hard, into the wall. (See Figure 30.) The ball will come off the wall at an angle toward your middle man. You must be ready, because it really flies off the wall. As the ball comes off the wall, smash it into the goal with your middle man.

At first you will probably completely miss the ball as it comes off the wall. Keep working at it; it is all a matter of timing. The more you work at it, the easier it becomes.

Three-Man-to-Five-Man Reverse Smash

This shot is rather difficult and will require a little more practice to master. Begin with the ball backpinned on the three-man row right around the dot. Position your five row so the center man on the five row is in line with the center man on the three-man where the ball is pinned. (See Figure 31A.) Now, without moving the ball, position your hand on the handle, with your fingertips on the edge (as in Figure 31B). Now, roll your hand down the handle, causing your man to make one revolution clockwise. This will hit the ball backward to the spot where your five-man is waiting. You then smash the ball into the goal with your center man on the five-man row. (See Figure 31C.)

TRICK SHOTS 103

(31A)

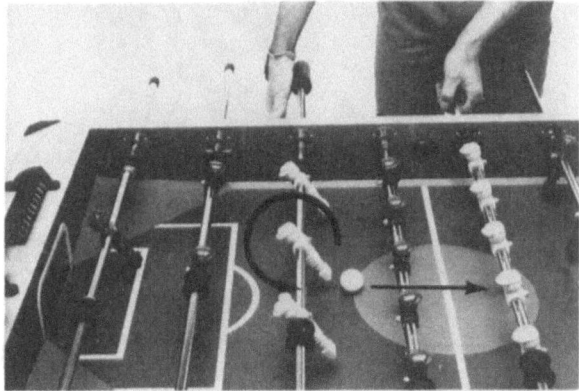
(31B)

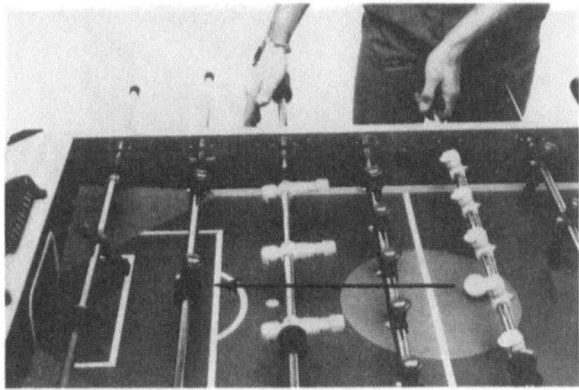
(31C)

Figure 31A–31C: 3 man–5 man reverse smash

104　THE COMPLETE BOOK OF FOOSBALL

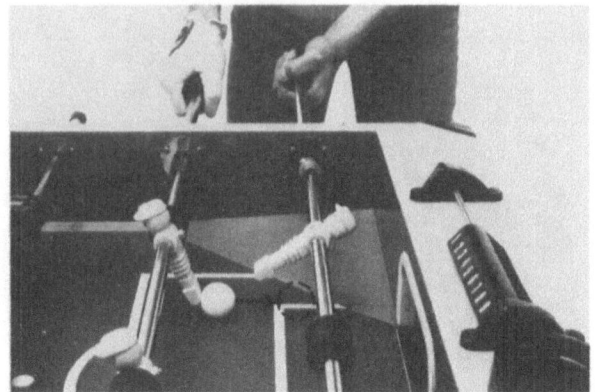

(32A)

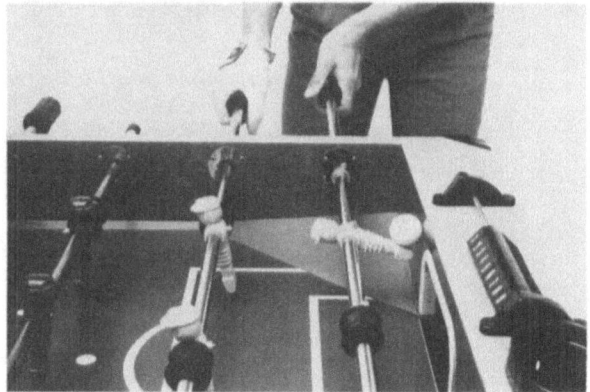

(32B)

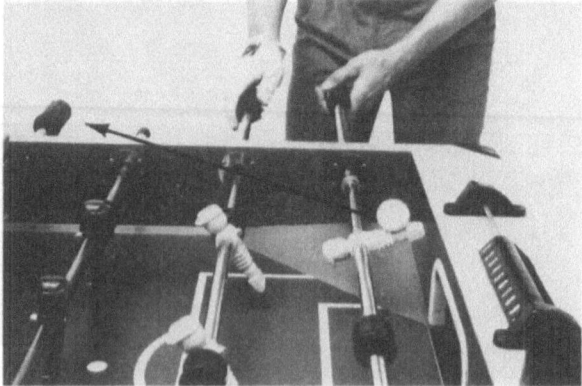

(32C)

Figure 32A-32C: Goalie field

GOALIE POSITION

Two-Man-to-One-Man Reverse Smash

Backpin the ball in the center of the table with either the near or the far man on the two-man rod. Position the one-man goalie directly behind the ball. Now, using the same hand motion as described earlier on the three-man-to-five-man smash, pass the ball back to the goalie, who in turn shoots the ball on goal.

Once you have this down, instead of shooting with the goalie, try passing the ball back to the two-man and then shooting.

Goalie Field Goal Attempt

This shot is very difficult to master and requires much practice. However, it is truly one of the most amazing shots I have ever seen and is well worth the time if you want to learn a trick shot from the goalie position.

Begin with the ball backpinned just outside the goal (as in Figure 32A). The one-man goalie should be directly in line with the ball, but its foot should be tipped forward high enough for the ball to pass underneath.

The object is to hit the ball backward and let it pass under the goalie. As it passes under the goalie, you make an attempt to move the goalie's foot back, catching the ball up on the backwall (as in Figure 32B). As you can imagine, this is not easy and requires much practice. Once you have the ball in this position, you can then try to shoot it on goal. Simply flip the ball through the air toward the opponent's goal. (See Figure 32C.) With practice, you should get it near the goal every time. This shot is tough to master and should never be tried in a tournament game.

10
Game Variations

When foosers get together just to have some fun, they almost always end up at the foosball table. However, most players who are just out to enjoy themselves and have a good time will play a faster type of game in which the ball is kept in continuous motion until someone scores. Usually referred to as rollerball, it is fast-paced and exciting, and a player must rely more on reflexes than brains.

There are many game variations on a foosball table that provide a pleasant break from serious tournament competition. The following rules are for a few of the more popular games played by many players across the country. Try playing them with your friends. Not only are they fun, but they also provide an excellent way to develop your reflexes, timing, and sheer speed on the foosball table.

FOUR ON FOUR (OR FOUR-MAN)

This is a great game to play when you have lots of players and only one table. It's guaranteed lots of fun, and a must for foos parties.

GAME VARIATIONS 107

Four-on-four

Rules

1. Each team consists of four players. Each player controls one rod with one hand only, but it may be either the left or the right hand.
2. A coin toss determines who serves first, as in conventional games. The player controlling the five-man row may serve to himself or have another member of the team drop the ball for him.
3. Points are scored in the conventional manner.
4. Rotation (forward one position, with the player at the three-man going to the back to the one-man) is required each time your team scores a point. Then, and only then, can rotation occur. Players must always stay in the same order as they started.
5. Four on Four is rocketball. This means that the ball may be stationary for *one* second and no longer, and shooting from a pin position is not allowed. A player may pin a moving ball

momentarily to gain control of it, but the ball must then touch another man before it is shot. There is a ten-second rod limit.
6. The first team to score five points wins the game.

THREE ON THREE (OR THREE-MAN)

Similar to Four Man, but using only three players, this is also a good game for parties.

Rules

1. Each team consists of three players. Each player controls one rod with one hand only, but it may be either the left or the right hand.
2. One rod will always be left idle, but players may jump from rod to rod, even while the ball is in play, as long as they stay in order (no crossing of hands) and as long as they use only one hand at all times.
3. In all other ways, Three on Three is played just like Four on Four. Rotation is allowed only after scoring a point, and then it is mandatory. Like Four on Four, Three on Three is rocketball. (See Four on Four rules for rocketball time limits.)

TWO-BALL ROLLERBALL

This game is not only fun, but it's also excellent for developing reflexes and hand-eye coordination.

Rules

1. Each team serves a ball on the count of three.
2. There is a ten-second rod possession time limit with a three-second stop or pin limit.
3. The team that scores the first ball has two options:
    A. They can take one point if they can get control (posses-

sion) of the second ball. If the opposing team scores the second ball before the other team can get possession of it, there is no score for either team.

B. The team that scores the first ball may choose to go for two points instead of one by attempting to score the second ball. Again, if the second ball is scored by the other team, the point for the first ball is canceled. The team that scores the first ball may decide to play the second ball, but always has the option to say that they want to stop play and take the one point for the first ball at any time that the second ball is in their possession.

4. The first team to get five points wins the game.

GOALIE WAR

With every major tournament now featuring both novice and professional goalie war events, this has become not only a popular game, but also a very profitable one to practice and play. A must for you goalies out there.

Rules

STARTING THE MATCH

1. Match play begins the same as in conventional games with a coin flip. The player winning the serve will release the ball from one of his corners. You must touch *two* men before shooting. (This holds true even when a dead ball is re-served.)
2. Serves thereafter go to the player last scored upon.

POSSESSION

1. This is the basis of goalie war rules. If player A takes a shot and it enters the opposing goalie's zone, but player B fails to control it and, consequently, the ball stops near the middle out of reach of both players, then player A retains possession and re-serves.
2. However, if player A shoots the ball and the shot does not

One of the top goalies, Ken Rivera, warms up for a big match in goalie war.

enter the opposing player's zone, then player B obtains possession and re-serves. This is true even if the ball goes airborne and hits the three- or five-man rod and returns to the original shooter's zone. In this instance, player B would still receive the ball.

The ball must *enter* and *leave* a player's zone before he loses possession.

3. A shot is defined as any ball leaving the reach of a player's two-man rod, whether intentional or not. If a player is maneuvering the ball between his two-man rod and his goalie and loses control out of reach of his two-man rod, this is considered a shot and the opposing goalie re-serves the ball.
4. A player's zone is defined as the area in back of the two-man rod but *includes* the area in front of that rod where he can reach the ball with an extended man.

BALL LEAVING TABLE

1. If the ball leaves the table, it goes back to the original server.

TIME

1. There is a ten-second total goalie possession limit with a three-second stopped or pinned ball rule.

TWO ON ONE

This is a game variation, and is excellent practice for all facets of your game, especially your singles play.

Rules

1. Two players on one side play as a normal doubles team, while a single player on the opposite side plays both sets of rods as in singles.
2. Only the single player may receive a point when he or she scores a ball. When one of the players on the doubles side scores, then all the players must rotate. Rotation is as follows: The single player goes to goalie on the doubles side. The doubles goalie goes to forward, and the doubles forward becomes the singles player on the opposite side.
3. Points are accumulated only by a player when playing alone until someone scores five points.
4. When the lone player scores, he receives the point and does not rotate until one of the doubles players scores a goal.

11
Common Rules and Etiquette

Before the arrival of national tournament competition, the rules of the game were few and simple. As players began to take the game more seriously and prize money increased, these vague rules were easily abused.

Tournament competition quickly bred a new kind of player—calculating, shrewd, and determined to win. With this new breed of player came the need for a set of precise, carefully worded rules. If your goal is to compete in tournament play, you should definitely study and learn the complete rules of foosball. The official WTSA Rules of Play can be found at the end of this book in Appendix I. If you are a beginner, or you just enjoy playing foosball for the fun of it, you may not feel that it is necessary to learn each and every detailed rule. All players should be aware of the following common rules and courtesies in order to play an enjoyable yet fair game of foosball.

RULES
The Serve

One of the main rules that beginners should know about is the rule governing the serve. Many amateur players believe that it is illegal to influence the direction of the ball on the serve. This is *not* true. In fact, the smart player serves the ball so that it rolls to his or her five-man every time. The reason for this is to prevent either player from gaining an unfair advantage. Each time a player scores, the opponent gets the next serve. The first serve of a game should be made by the team that lost the preceding game. In the case of a challenge, the challenger receives the first serve.

Spinning

Spinning the rods is illegal! Spinning is defined as the rotation of any playing figure more than 360 degrees (one revolution) either before or after striking the ball. For example, if you have the ball in a frontpin and you want to shoot it straight, it is legal to spin the playing figure backward, hitting the ball on the way down, because the playing figure has traveled less than one revolution before striking the ball.

Five-Man Play

A stopped or pinned ball on the five-man cannot be passed directly to the three-man rod of the same team. It must first touch at least two playing figures on the five row before being passed. In other words, play on the five-man rod should be almost continuous. The ball may be stopped momentarily (three seconds), but must be put back into motion quickly.

Ball Out of Play

If the ball should leave the playing area and strike the scoring markers, ash trays, formica on top of the side rails and cabinet ends, or any object that is not part of the table, and then return into the playing area, it shall be declared out of play. The ball should be put back into play with a serve by the team that originally served it.

Dead Ball

A ball is considered dead when it cannot be reached by any playing figure. A dead ball between the goal and the nearest two-man rod is put back into play by the goalie, who drops the ball from the nearest corner.

If the ball is dead between the two two-man rods, it is reserved by the team that originally served the ball.

In-and-Out

A ball that enters the goal and bounces back out is considered the same as a point scored. The point counts and the next ball is served.

Changing Positions

When playing doubles, the players must remain in position until the point is scored. Players may switch positions between points or between games.

Distractions

Any movement or sound away from the rod where the ball is in play may be judged a distraction. A distraction is illegal. This includes moving the five-man rod to distract the goalie as you shoot from the three-man, shouting as you shoot the ball, etc.

Reaching In

It is illegal to reach into the play area anytime while the ball is in play. This includes setting the ball in place by hand or reaching into the goal to try to retrieve a shot.

FOOSBALL ETIQUETTE

Written rules can be defined and enforced; there also exists,

COMMON RULES AND ETIQUETTE 115

Win or lose, foosers have learned to react with good sportsmanship.

however, an unwritten code of ethics among players that is based on good sportsmanship. The national tour has demanded, and received, professionalism from the players. The effect of this effort to upgrade the image of the sport and the players has reached even the local level. Basic courtesy and good sportsmanship have become integral parts of the game. The following guidelines explain some of the customs of foosball, helping the beginner become a more courteous player.

1. If you want to play, but there are no free tables, the proper procedure is to challenge a table by placing enough money for the price of one game on the end of the table. If you want to play doubles, you should challenge a table at which the players are already playing doubles. If you want to play singles, challenge a singles game. There may be other challenges ahead of you; if so, you must wait for your turn. When it is your turn, you will play against the team or player who just won. If you win, you may continue to play, taking on the next challenger. It is customary for the challenger to receive the first serve.

2. Smokers should be careful that their smoking does not bother the opponent. Smoking is not allowed during tournament play, so a good habit to develop is to avoid smoking while playing. If you do smoke, be sure to use the ashtrays provided. Food and drinks should also be kept away from the table. A little care can keep a table in good condition for a long time.

3. It is considered common courtesy to avoid distracting your opponent while playing. Loud talking, banging the rods, etc., while your opponent is shooting are not only distractions and therefore illegal, but are characteristic of a discourteous player and a poor sport.

4. Learn to cope with losing as well as winning. No player can win all the time, so you must be able to control your frustrations—and your temper. Have respect for the property you are on, the equipment you are using, and the people around you. You will probably use the same foosball table week after week, so don't abuse it out of lack of self-control.

5. Be a courteous spectator as well as player. When watching a match, give the players plenty of room. Cheering for your favorite team is fine, but shouting will distract both teams. Remember that spectators are not allowed to call shots or coach a player during a game while the ball is in play. Spectators can speak to players during time-outs and between games.

More and more people are discovering foosball every day. They may become avid players or remain interested spectators; either way, the image they form of our sport is the one conveyed by you, the player, on an everyday basis. Think of yourself as an ambassador for foosball. Wherever you go, you represent our sport, so always be courteous and exhibit good sportsmanship.

12
Tournament Competition

There is no better method to improve your foosball game than participating in competition. Whether it's playing in a small draw-your-partner tournament or participating on a city league team, the valuable exposure to serious competition can improve your game quicker than any other way. In competition you will learn how to react to different situations, how to play under pressure, and, most important of all, how your opponents play. Which shots, passes, and defenses do they prefer? Just observing competition can be very rewarding. Watch the team that is winning the tournament. Why are they winning? Are they more calm, more aggressive, faster, smarter? Beginners should measure their experience at a tournament not by how high they placed, but by how much they learned. Be alert, watch the better players, and don't be afraid to ask questions. Try to get as much knowledge out of each tournament as you possibly can. If you place high, great; if not, chalk it up to experience and go on to the next tournament, knowing that you are a better player than before.

LOCAL COMPETITION

Today, local foosball tournaments and league competition can be found in nearly every region of the United States. Many cities have gamerooms and taverns that specialize in foosball, running weekly and monthly tournaments. Some cities, such as Seattle, St. Louis, and Portland, Oregon, have player associations that organize and run city competition, as well as keep their members informed about local and national foosball through monthly newsletters.

Find out if there is a player association in your town. If there is, become an active member. League competition welcomes beginners, so don't worry about your level of skill. Enter draw-your-partner events. This gives beginners a chance to draw a good partner and gain that valuable tournament experience. If your favorite foosball establishment does not run tournaments or sponsor a league team, you should offer your help to the management and get them involved in organized competition.

If there are no tournaments or leagues in your area, get something started. Talk to the other local foosball players and to the managers of foosball arenas. If you need assistance, contact the World Table Soccer Association. Tournament charts, instructions on how to run tournaments, and league guidelines are available to help you.

COLLEGE TOURNAMENTS

Each year, the Associated College Unions–International (ACU-I), in conjunction with Tournament Soccer, holds a national amateur championship. Colleges across the country hold tournaments, and the winners from each campus then compete on a regional level. The regional winners receive an expense-paid trip to the ACU-I national championships held at one of the major professional tournaments during spring each year.

If you are a college student, you should check with your student union game center to find out whether your school is

1979 Collegiate finalists Intercollegiate Association of College Unions, Minneapolis, Minnesota.

participating in the ACU-I program. If more information is needed, the ACU-I may be contacted through the WTSA.

PROFESSIONAL TOURNAMENTS

Imagine the grand ballroom of an elegant hotel, with crystal chandeliers, plush carpeting, and colorful tournament posters and banners. Add to that a hundred brand-new foosball tables, arranged neatly in rows and numbered for match identification, plus two pit foosball tables, surrounded by bleachers to accommodate enthusiastic spectators. Fill that ballroom with a thousand eager foosball players, and fill the air with excitement. If you can imagine all of this, then you have an idea of what a professional tournament is like.

The chances are good that each year the professional tour will make a stop somewhere near you, maybe even in your city. You may be thinking that, since you are not a professional player, the tour is not for you. Wrong! The professional level of

Ballroom action at the 1979 $250,000 World Championships.

competition is only one part of the excitement of a tour tournament. There are novice events, rookie events, women's events, draw your partners, state team challenge matches, pro-am events, clinics, player hospitality suites, buffets, and much, much more. It is a chance not only to compete, but also to have a good time doing it.

RANKING OF PLAYERS

At a tour tournament, players are classified according to their skill level. As the sport of foosball has grown and the prize money has increased, the standards used to determine a player's ranking have evolved accordingly. A major change in the classification system went into effect January 1, 1980. For the first time, a player could have one status in a category, such as singles novice, but have a different status in a second category, such as doubles pro. As of January 1, 1980, the various player classifications are as follows.

Rookie: the lowest classification, designed for the beginner or inexperienced player. Any player who has won $50 in a category may no longer play at the rookie level.

Novice: the status of a player who is more experienced than a rookie but has not yet won $400 or more in the category in question.

Pro: the status of an experienced tour player who has won at least $400 in the category in question.

Master: the highest status in any one category, given to the pro player who has earned more than $2,000 in that category.

The many different events at a tour tournament have been divided into three categories for the purpose of determining the rank of players. The doubles category includes the following events: championship (master) doubles, pro doubles, novice doubles, and rookie doubles. The singles category is made up of championship singles, pro singles, novice singles, and rookie singles. The third category is called other, and it is comprised of all other events, including championship and novice mixed doubles, championship and novice women's doubles, women's singles, and championship and novice goalie war.

Once a player has attained a certain ranking, he may not compete at a lower level of play, but always has the option to enter a higher level if he so chooses. For instance, a novice doubles player may enter novice doubles, pro doubles, or even try his luck against the masters in championship doubles, but he may not enter rookie doubles.

The total of tour prize money for all players returns to zero on January 1 each year, but the ranking of a player upon entering the new year is determined by the amount of prize money won in the year that just ended. For example, a player who ends the year with a doubles category total of more than $400 but less than $2,000, and has therefore achieved pro status in that category, starts the new year with a prize money total of zero but keeps the pro ranking in that category.

At the point during the year at which a player reaches the required amount of money to upgrade his status, the new status goes into effect immediately after the tournament at which it happened. The only time that a player's ranking can change to a lower status is at the first of the year. For example, a player who has turned pro in singles in 1979 will be ranked no lower than a pro in 1980. If he wins more than $2,000 in singles during 1980, he will upgrade his status to master, effective at the time it happens. If, however, he wins less than $400 in singles during 1980, he will return to novice status in that category on January 1, 1981, and will retain that ranking until he has again won more than $400 to turn professional again.

If this sounds very confusing, don't worry. If you have never played in a tour tournament, you are automatically ranked as a rookie, and all classifications of play are open to you. If you have played on the tour and would like to check your current status, contact the WTSA. Lists of pro and master players on the tour are regular features in *Foos Noos*, the official publication of the WTSA.

TOURNAMENT EVENTS

Besides the main events at a tour tournament, such as doubles, singles, and mixed doubles, there are many specialty events. Most of the players who travel to tournaments will enter at least two main events, but for those players who are eliminated early, or for those who just can't seem to get enough foos, the specialty events offer another chance to win some prize money and get some tournament experience. Standard at most tour tournaments are the Friday night draw your partner, goalie war, and a second-chance draw your partner on the last day of the tournament. Some offer pro-am, rollerball, or four on four events for variety. Because both the pressure and the entry fees are lower in the specialty events, it makes sense for the player desiring experience to enter as many as possible. No matter what the skill level or experience factors in your game, there are many events at a tour tournament that you can enter *and* be competitive in.

Tour events are open to everyone. All you need to enter an event is the posted entry fee. Occasionally, a special regional tournament will be open only to qualifiers from that region, but the general rule for all tour events is that they are open to all,

CLEVELAND AND SYRACUSE $50,000 SPECTACULARS HIGHLIGHT $300,000 FALL TOUR

PRIZE MONEY BREAKDOWN

	Champ. Doubles	Pro Doubles	Novice Doubles	Rookie Doubles		Champ. Singles	Pro Singles	Novice Singles	Womens Singles	Rookie Singles		Open Goalie War	Second Chance Open DYP*	Second Chance Novice or Lady DYP**	$300 DYP
1	4000	1000	300	Trophy	1	1000	300	150	100	Trophy	1		800	250	100
2	3000	800	250	Trophy	2	800	250	100	80	Trophy	2		600	180	60
3	2000	500	200	Trophy	3	600	200	80	60	Trophy	3		400	120	50
4	1000	300	140	—	4	400	160	70	40	—	4		200	100	40
5/6	600	250	100		5/6	300	120	60	30		5/6		100	80	25
7/8	400	200	75		7/8	200	80	50	10		7/8		80	60	—
9/12	300	150	60		9/12	100	40	30			9/12		60	40	
13/16	200	100	50		13/16	—	30	20			13/16			20	
17/24	—	—	40												
Entry Fee Per Player:	$100	$50	$15	$2		$75	$30	$10	$10	$2			$30	$10	$3

		Champ. Mixed Doubles	Novice Mixed Doubles	Rookie Mixed Doubles		Champ. Womens Doubles	Novice Womens Doubles	Rookie Womens Doubles		Open Goalie War	Novice or Lady Goalie War**	
	1	800	200	Trophy	1	700	200	Trophy	1	300	200	*No Two Pros Together.
	2	600	100	Trophy	2	400	100	Trophy	2	200	100	
	3	400	80	Trophy	3	300	80	Trophy	3	150	70	**Novice Ladies Get One Point Spot per Game.
	4	300	60	—	4	200	60	—	4	100	60	
	5/6	250	50		5/6	150	40		5/6	80	40	
	7/8	200	40		7/8	100	30		7/8	60	30	
	9/12		30		9/12	—	20		9/12	40	20	
	13/16		20						13/16	—	10	
	Entry Fee Per Player:	$50	$15	$2		$40	$15	$2		$30	$10	

Sample prize money and entry fee breakdown from a $50,000 tournament.

with no qualifications. Even at the prestigious world championships, your entry fee is all that is required in order for you to have a shot at becoming the next world champion.

PROFESSIONAL INSTRUCTION

A regular feature at all professional tournaments is the pro player's clinic, offering professional instruction to all present, free of charge. These clinics cover all aspects of the game and are followed by a question-and-answer session. When you attend a tournament, be sure to check the schedule of events to see when the clinic will take place—then don't miss it! You will witness a top money winner demonstrating and talking about the things he or she does best—the skills and strategies that put this player at the top. You can benefit greatly by attending the pro player's clinic, for the small price of an hour of your time.

A proper understanding of the basic techniques is essential if you intend to become a good player. You can spend several hours a day practicing, but if you are not developing good habits and practicing correct technique, you will not become a successful player. This book can give you a solid foundation, but as you progress, you will undoubtedly seek more instruction.

Most advanced players are flattered when someone turns to them for guidance. If you have a problem with some part of your game, a more experienced player may be able to give you a tip that will solve it for you. Watch carefully, ask questions, and listen attentively. The advice you receive can help your game grow in the right direction.

Many professional players give private lessons. If there is a pro player in your area, there is a very good chance that he or she would be interested in setting up a program of private instruction for you.

TOURNAMENT PROCEDURES

Players are sometimes reluctant to go to their first big tournament simply because they are unfamiliar with the procedures to register and play. The following guidelines should answer any questions you might have about going to a tournament, registering, and competing.

Before You Go

HOTEL RESERVATIONS

The hotel hosting the foosball tournament usually reserves a block of rooms for the foosball players and offers them a special group rate. You should make your reservations at least three weeks in advance and be sure to specify that you are with the foosball group. Otherwise, they may tell you that no rooms are available, or they may charge you the full rate.

TRAVEL

Now that you have your hotel reservations, all you need to do is get there. The most common means of transportation for foosball players is by car or plane; however, train, bus, and thumb are other alternatives. Whatever type of transportation you decide to use, be sure to make your plans or reservations well in advance. If you are going by car, be sure to allow yourself plenty of time so that you don't miss any events. Contact other players and drive together—it's more fun and less expensive. If you are traveling by plane or bus, making your reservations early can sometimes save you as much as 50 percent of your fare. Travel agencies cost you nothing and can help you save money.

DRESS CODE

As you prepare for the tournament, be sure that the clothes you take with you to play in are acceptable according to the WTSA dress code. Improper attire may be cause for forfeiture of game, games, or match. The code is as follows.

1. Professional players are required to wear a shirt with a collar (golf or coach's shirt style) with the player's name embroidered or permanently printed over the right pocket. Novice and rookie players are not required to wear shirts with collars and their names, but are encouraged to do so.

2. Slacks or dress jeans should be worn. No shorts or ragged jeans are acceptable.

3. Shoes must be worn. No sandals without socks.

4. Visors with a modest brim are allowed, but not hats.

TIME SCHEDULE

Time of events may vary due to schedule changes at some tournaments. Not all tournaments follow the same schedule. Know in advance when entries for each event close. Look for tournament schedules in *Foos Noos* or on posters at your favorite foosball location.

Once You Have Arrived

You have survived the trip there and you're all fired up to start foosin'. So where are the tables?

THE TOURNAMENT ROOM

At most events, the tournament is held in the main ballroom of the hotel. But wait—the tournament room normally does not open until 6:00 P.M. on the first day of the tournament. Up to that time, the tournament crew is working hard to take care of last-minute details, and players wandering in and out of the room are most unwelcome. On the following days, the room opens at 9:00 A.M.—in plenty of time to warm up for the full day of foosball ahead.

REGISTRATION

You must be present at the tournament site to register. There is no preregistration by phone or mail. When signing up for a particular event, you have thirty minutes before the posted starting time to register. Be sure to fill out the registration form completely and legibly. This is important because your name and address will then be added to the mailing list to receive information about future tournaments. To avoid standing in long lines, sign up as soon as possible after the registration booth opens.

Are you a WTSA member? This question appears on all entry forms and determines whether you must pay the surcharge assessed to nonmembers. If you are a member, show your membership card with your entry form. This expedites the registration process immensely. If you are not a member, you should consider joining at the tournament. Besides supporting the WTSA and receiving a one-year subscription to *Foos Noos*, you will not have to pay the nonmember surcharge. (All surcharges go to pay officiating fees.)

Charts and Cards, or When Do I Play?

After registration closes for an event, it is normally at least one-half hour before the charts are drawn and the match cards written. Before the first-round matches are called, all teams receiving "byes" will be announced. If you receive a bye, that means you have automatically won your first match. But listen closely—your next match will be called shortly.

MATCH CARDS

After the charts are filled in, the individual matches are written on match cards. Each match will be announced over the PA system, and as they are called, the match card is punched on a time clock in order to record the starting time. These cards are then displayed in the plexiglass match card tree at the front of the stage. Normally, these cards are color-coded for particular events. Your match card will be placed in the numbered slot on the card tree that corresponds to the number on the table your match is on. If you are not sure of your table number, check the match card tree, but don't take the card out!

RECALL CARDS

If your opponents don't show up, don't be alarmed. Be sure you are in the right place, first of all, and if you are, wait three minutes. If the opponents haven't shown up after three minutes, go to the stage and fill out a recall card. Write the team name of your opponent, the number of the table, and the name of the event (e.g., pro doubles). Then place the card in the plastic bin. If your opponent fails to answer the first recall, he forfeits the first game. Failure to answer the second recall means forfeiture of the entire match.

NUTS-AND-BOLTS CARDS AND OFFICIAL CARDS

If your table needs repairs (nuts and bolts) or if an official is needed to make a ruling, fill out the appropriate card, place the card in the bin, then return to your table and wait.

What to Do When Your Match Is Over

IF YOU WIN

When the match is over, the winning team must come to the

match card tree, pull their card out of the corresponding numbered slot, and sign their team name as it appears on the card. *Do not change your team name* when you sign the card (unless you have been instructed by the tournament crew to shorten your name, usually in the case of a draw-your-partner event). Place your signed match card in the bin—*not back in the card tree*. Your next match will be called shortly.

IF YOU LOSE

Don't leave after your first loss! Most events at a tournament are double elimination, which means that you must lose twice to be eliminated from that event. Wait and listen—your next match will be called soon.

Rules of Conduct

1. No smoking, eating, or drinking is allowed in the tournament room.

2. Behavior: Ninety-nine percent of all players display good manners and respect at tournament hotel sites. However, that 1 percent can ruin it for the rest of the players. In order for foosball to be recognized as a first-class professional sport, the players must act in a first-class professional manner. If a player is caught damaging hotel property or has not paid a hotel bill, he or she will not be allowed to participate in future tournaments until the situation is rectified.

VIEWING A MATCH

When watching a match, please give the players plenty of room to play, and don't do or say things that might distract them. Consideration and sportsmanship are the key words here.

Congratulations! You Placed In The Money!

Checks and trophies may be picked up at the stage usually by

3:00 P.M. on the final day of the tournament. The top three teams in all main events receive trophies or plaques. Many times pictures are desired for *Foos Noos* and other media. Your cooperation is appreciated.

Player Responsibilities

1. Be aware of registration closing times and all schedule changes.
2. Be on time for your matches. An alarm clock comes in handy in case the hotel forgets your wake-up call.
3. Listen carefully to all announcements.
4. Remember to sign your match card after winning.
5. Know and comply with the WTSA Dress Code and WTSA Rules of Play.
6. Do not interrupt the announcer.
7. Do not leave the tournament area between matches.

13
Women's Competition

As the sport of foosball grows, more and more women are becoming avid players. On national as well as local levels, women are learning that foosball is more a game of brains and experience than of physical strength. Many women today are able to hold their own against male players and are placing high in the open categories of tournament competition.

One of the best foosball players of all time, Lori Schranz, stands a mere five feet tall. A six-time world champion, Lori has won more major titles than any player, male or female, and is living proof of a woman's ability to compete in head-to-head competition against men.

Female players tend to lean more toward a finesse style of play, since they don't always have the strength of the men. What top female players may lack in power and strength, they make up through quick, smooth shots and calm, intelligent play.

As far as playing techniques are concerned, the mechanics of foosball are the same for both men and women. In fact, many women feel that foosball is the ideal sport for them, since it allows them to compete on an equal level with men.

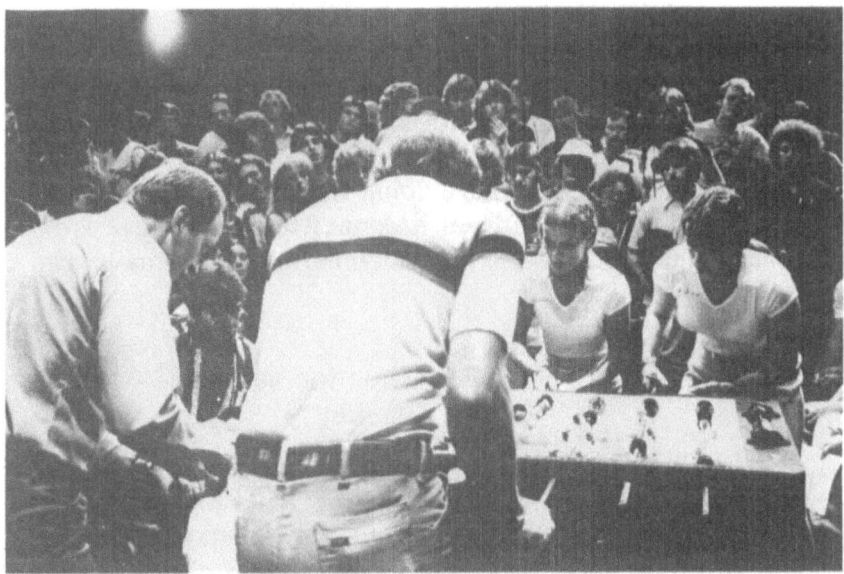

Top women's team Lori Schranz and Karin Gililland in finals of 1978 $100,000 Super Doubles.

At every major tournament, there are special categories for women in both singles and doubles. This is an excellent arrangement for female foosers, because they have the choice of playing in the women's categories, in the open categories, or in both. The mixed doubles event is also very popular and can serve as a stepping-stone for women players who wish to advance from the women's categories to the open categories. You could say that women have the advantage at tournaments, since they are able to compete in almost every event, if they so choose. Each year more women are playing foosball, some because it is fun and pleasurable, and some because it is a serious alternative in the world of professional sports.

Pro Tip for Women—Lori Schranz

Women often have the attitude of "I can't do that." If you really want to do something, you can! You shouldn't feel intimidated when you play someone who is better than you are. In fact, you should practice and play as often as possible against more experienced players.

Watch the better players and try to copy the techniques they use. Don't be shy or afraid to ask for advice on a shot or defense. This way you don't waste your time learning improper techniques or developing bad habits. If you stick with it and don't let yourself become frustrated, there is no limit to the level of skill that anyone, male or female, can attain.

Pro Tip on the Pull Shot for Women— Carrie Crowell

To shoot my pull shot, I begin by concentrating on total relaxation of the muscles in my arm. I like to use a loose grip on the handle, because it gives me a better feel for the contact between the arm and the ball. A smooth but snappy takeoff is essential for a good shot, and you must have a good feel for the ball to achieve it.

The smart player doesn't have to have a "killer" long pull shot. This is especially important for women players. The player who has a good inside game and can shoot all of the options, including an accurate long, will be a successful shooter. There are five holes for the pull shot shooter: the straight or one-hole; the two-hole, which is just past the straight; the three-hole, which is the dot; the four-hole, which is just past the dot; and the five-hole, which is the long.

The best shooter is one who strives for perfection in all five of the options. The moving straight is a *must* for the player who does not have a devastating long. The key to the moving straight is the takeoff—it must be quick and smooth. The short split to the two-hole is also a very effective option. Try not to worry about scoring the long. Play smart. Use all of the options, and don't forget to vary your timing before takeoff. Then believe that you're good, shoot with confidence, and you will be successful.

14
Bridging the Communication Gap

Anytime something grows as fast and becomes as popular as foosball has in the last few years, a communication gap is bound to develop between the broad base of novice players and the more serious tournament players. Today, for every player who is aware of the competitive level of foosball and the degree of skill involved in the game, there are a hundred people who enjoy playing foosball yet have little understanding of the game, the rules, or the techniques that can be developed on a foosball table.

By purchasing this book, you have taken a giant step toward becoming a more knowledgeable and skillful player. You now know what techniques you should develop—all that remains is for you to practice and learn how to use them. Only so much can be learned from a book. You now must spend hours and hours of practice working to adapt the many different techniques to your own style of play.

Today, as a foosball player, you are especially fortunate. With the expanded number of players and tournaments throughout the country, you should be able to locate foosball leagues and tournaments in your area. You may even find a local professional who will give you pointers and advice on your game. The first thing you need to do is to contact the World Table Soccer Association (WTSA). Try to find out if there is a local foosball association in your area. If so, become a member. It usually costs very little, and the valuable playing experience and information you will receive are well worth the dues. You should also consider becoming a member of the WTSA, especially if there is no local association. You need not be a pro to join, and membership includes a one-year subscription to *Foos Noos*, the official magazine of the WTSA, featuring news of upcoming tournaments in your area and throughout the nation, plus valuable pro tips on the latest techniques and shots.

Formed in 1975, the WTSA is the official sanctioning association of the professional tour. The WTSA provides the officials for all sanctioned tournaments. Besides a subscription to *Foos Noos*, WTSA membership also includes reduced rates on officiating surcharges at tournaments. At the time of this writing, membership costs $15 per year. For information, write: WTSA, P.O. Box 80605, Seattle, WA 98108, or call toll-free, 800-426-8897.

Should you decide to take up foosball seriously, you have at your disposal the tools to become the next world champion. If you practice, stay in touch, compete, and continue to improve, you too can earn a living as a professional foosball player. Even if you are an occasional player who loves the game and enjoys it as a hobby, you can play an important role in the development of our sport. When you go out to play, spread the word of the sport of foosball and be willing to spend a minute or two to show a beginner a shot or explain a rule. With your help, foosball will continue to grow, both locally and professionally, and to offer fun and excitement for beginners and pros alike.

Appendix I:
WTSA Rules of Play

1979 RULES

1. To Start a Match

1.1 A coin flip shall decide the team with the choice of table side or first serve. The team that loses the flip shall have the remaining option and pay for the first game, with that expense alternating with each game.

1.2 In the event of the loser's bracket winner beating the winner's bracket team in the first match, the second match will be started in the same manner as a regular match with the coin flip, etc.

2. The Serve

2.1 The ball shall be put into play to start a match or after a point is scored by a serve through the serving hole. The server may attempt to influence the roll of the ball, but may not allow any part of either hand to enter the play area. The play area shall be defined as the area above the playing surface to the height of the side boards of the cabinet.

2.2 While the server may not allow any part of either hand to enter the play area while serving, he may put either hand in the play area to put the ball in position for his serve, prior to releasing the ball into play. If the ball falls into the play area while the server is doing this, he must pick it up and re-serve it. If he drops it again at any time during that match, he loses the serve to the opposing team.

2.3 The ball may not be struck by either team following a serve until it has touched the playfield, at which time the ball is considered to be "in play."

2.4 Spinning the ball shall be allowed in order to influence the serve; however, no point shall be scored by the serving team unless the ball is struck by one of the serving team's player figures.

2.5 The server must signify that play is about to begin by tapping the ball on the side of the table. The server must not serve the ball until he has assurance that the opposing team is ready for play to begin.

2.6 In the event of a violation of any part of this rule, the opposing team shall have the option of continuing play from the point of infraction or having the ball re-served by the original server. The second violation shall result in the ball being put into play by a serve of the opposing team.

3. Subsequent Serves

3.1 Following the first serve of a match, subsequent serves shall be made by the team last scored upon. First serves in subsequent games of a multigame match shall be made by the team which lost the preceding game.

3.2 If the ball is served by the wrong team, and the violation is discovered before the ball is scored, play shall be stopped, and the ball shall be re-served by the proper team. Once the ball is scored, no protests shall be allowed, and play shall continue as if no infraction had been committed.

3.3 If a team receives the serve due to the opposing team being penalized for a rules infraction, and if after the ball is served, it goes dead or leaves the table, it is re-served by the person who originally served it prior to the infraction.

4. Ball in Play

4.1 Once a ball is put into play by the server (*see* 2.3), it shall remain in play until the ball is hit out of play, a dead ball is declared, or a point is scored.

4.1a A ball entering the serving cup and then returning to the play field is considered "in play."

5. Ball Out of Play

5.1 If the ball should leave the playing area and strike the scoring markers, ashtrays, formica on top of the side rails and cabinet ends, or any object that is not a part of the table, and then return to the playing area, it shall be declared out of play and put back into play by a serve of the team which originally served that ball.

6. Dead Ball

6.1 A ball shall be declared a dead ball when it has completely stopped its motion and is not within reach of any playing figure. A dead ball shall be put back into play in one of the following ways:

6.1a If the ball is declared dead between either goal and the nearest two-man rod, it shall be put back into play by the goalie by placing the ball in either corner and releasing it into play. The goalie must have assurance that opposing team is ready for play to continue before putting the ball back into play in this manner. Furthermore, the goalie must then move the ball from one playing figure to a second one before the motion of a shot or pass may begin.

6.1b If the ball is declared dead anywhere between the two two-man rods, it shall be put back into play with a serve by the team that originally served that ball.

6.1c If a player causes a dead ball to come back into play by moving the table or banging the rods, the opposing team shall have the option of continuing play or re-serving the ball from its serving hole.

6.1d If a playing figure is broken while in contact with the ball, play shall resume at that rod. The ball must touch two figures before the motion of a shot or pass may begin.

7. Time-Out

7.1 Each team is allowed two time-outs per game during which the players may leave the table. Such time-outs shall not exceed thirty seconds. Either team may take the full thirty seconds even if the team that called the time-out does not wish to take the full allotment. Each team can call only one time-out per ball. A time-out called between balls shall apply to the following ball to be played in counting time-outs per game.

7.2 A team may call a time-out at anytime when in possession of the ball. Either team member may call time-out when either he or his partner has the ball. However, if a team member calls time-out while his partner has possession of the ball, the time-out starts the moment it is called, and anything that happens, such as a shot or pass by the partner with the ball, shall not count once time-out is declared. **Ball must be stopped to call time-out. The penalty for calling a time-out while the ball is in motion shall be loss of possession. If the opposing team has possession, the request for a time-out while the ball is in motion may be judged as a distraction if an official is present.**

7.3 If not in possession of the ball, a team wanting time-out must request it of the team in possession. The team in possession must honor the request for time-out immediately, unless they are in the process of shooting or passing at that exact moment. However, until the team in possession acknowledges the time-out, the ball remains in play, and the team requesting the time-out should remain on defense until the other team acknowledges.

7.4 Time-out may not be called by either team if the ball is in motion. If the other team is in possession of the ball, a time-out may not be requested if the opposing player is in the process of shooting or passing.

7.5 A team shall be charged with a time-out if either player takes his hands from the handles and turns from the table while the ball is in play. However, a player can take his hands from the handles to wipe them off before a shot, as long as it doesn't take more than two or three seconds. However, if the ball is set up to shoot, the ten-second clock is running while the player wipes his hands. The team on defense should not relax if an opponent takes his hand(s) off the rod.

7.6 If the time taken during a time-out extends beyond thirty seconds without the approval of an authorized tournament official, the team which causes the delay may be charged with a technical foul or fouls.

7.7 **Following a Time-Out:** The ball shall be put back into play by the player who had possession when time-out was called, at the place where the ball was last in play. Before play may resume, this player must have assurance that the opposing team is ready for play to continue.

    7.7a MOVEMENT OF THE BALL DURING TIME-OUT: It is illegal to reach in and/or touch the ball during a time-out (*see* 13.1d). The penalty for this is loss of possession.

    It is also illegal to practice during a time-out (*see* 17.1). Any movement of the ball, however slight, may be considered as practice by an opponent. Therefore, the player in possession of the ball should avoid this by not placing his hand on the handle of the rod where the ball is until all other players are at the table, have their hands on the rods, and are ready to play. When the player with the ball has the assurance that all other players are ready, play may continue and the player with the ball may then put his hand on that handle.

PENALTY FOR MOVING THE BALL DURING A TIME-OUT: The standard penalty for practicing during a match (*see* 17.1) is a technical foul. However, in the case of the player in possession of the ball returning to the table after a time-out and then moving the ball before play has officially resumed, the penalty for the first violation shall be loss of possession and the ball will be served by the opposing forward. The penalty for the second violation, and any succeeding violations, will be a technical foul.

7.7b **TO RESUME PLAY:** After being assured that the other players are ready, the player with the ball must move the ball from one playing figure to another before the motion of a shot or a pass may begin.

Penalty for shooting or passing after a time-out without touching two men first is the opponent's choice of either continuing play or serving the ball.

7.8 A team calling more than two time-outs per game or calling a second time-out on the same ball shall be charged with an automatic technical foul. In the case of a team having already used their first time-out and then calling a second time-out on the same ball, they are charged not only with a technical foul, but they also forfeit that second time-out. This rule shall be enforced even if an official is not present.

7.9 A maximum of sixty seconds is allowed between games. Either team can request the full sixty seconds. If both teams acknowledge that they are ready to resume play before the full time is used, play shall continue and the remainder of that sixty seconds is then forfeited. Time-outs between games in addition to the free sixty-second break are not allowed and will be an automatic technical if called.

7.10 **"Official" Time-Out:** If a disagreement arises during the play of a match as to interpretation of these rules, a player or team may request time-out to get an official. This time-out does **not** count as one of the two time-outs allowed per team per game. To request an official, a player should go to the stage and fill out the appropriate card, then return to the table and wait for the official. Any player may request an official at any time during a game.

7.11 **Table Maintenance Time-Out:** Any necessary table maintenance, such as changing balls, tightening the men, etc., must be requested before the start of the match. To do this, a player should go to the stage and fill out a Nuts and Bolts card, then return to the table and wait. The only time that a player may call a table maintenance time-out during a match would be in the case of a sudden alteration to the table, such as a broken man, broken screw, crumbling bumper, bent rod, etc. A time-out for table maintenance does not count as one of the two time-outs allowed per game.

7.12 **Medical Time-Out:** A player or team may request a medical time-out. This request must be approved by the tournament director and two members of the WTSA Board, who will determine the length of the medical time-out, up to a maximum of sixty minutes. A player who is physically unable to continue playing after that time must forfeit the match.

8. Point Scored on an In-and-Out

8.1 A ball which enters the goal but returns to the playing surface and/or leaves the table still counts as a goal.

    8.1a If there is a controversy over whether or not the ball entered the goal, an official should be called.

9. Table Sides

9.1 At the end of each game, teams must switch sides of the table before play of the next game can begin.

10. Change of Positions

10.1 In any doubles event each player may play only the two

rods normally designated for his position. Once the ball is served, the players must play the same position until the ball is scored. Players may switch after a point is scored or between games.

11. Spinning

11.1 Spinning of the rods is illegal. Spinning is defined as the rotation of any soccer figure more than 360 degrees before or after striking the ball. In calculating the 360 degrees, you do not add the degrees spun prior to striking the ball. A ball which is advanced by an illegal spin is replayed as follows.
    11.1a If the ball goes in the goal, then it will not be counted as a point and will be put back into play by the goalie as if the ball had been declared a dead ball between the goal and the nearest two-man rod.
    11.1b If the ball does not go in the goal, the opposing team will have the option of continuing play or reserving that ball.

11.2 Spinning of a rod which does not advance and/or strike the ball does not constitute an illegal spin.
    11.2a If a player's spinning rod hits the ball backward into his own goal, it will count as a goal for the opposing team.
    11.2b Spinning of a rod away from the ball (when there is no possession) is not considered an illegal spin, but may be ruled as a distraction.

12. Jarring

12.1 Any jarring, sliding, or lifting of the table shall be illegal. Whether or not the table jarring is done intentionally or not is of no consequence. This call must be made by an official.
    12.1a It is not necessary for a player to lose the ball for jarring to be called on his opponent.

12.2 The penalty for violation of this rule during a (one) game is as follows.

12.2a First Offense: The opposing team has the option of continuing play or re-serving that ball, with two exceptions: **(1)** Should an illegal jar by an opponent cause a player to lose the ball from his three row, the ball will be awarded to that player's three row and play will continue; **(2)** should the ball be jarred while the player(s) attempts to gain possession (such as a pass to the three row), the official present will make a judgment regarding possession of the ball.

12.2b Second Offense: Technical foul (*see* Technical Fouls).

12.2c Third Offense: Technical foul.

12.2d Fourth Offense: Forfeiture of game.

12.3 In succeeding games of the same match, the penalty is as follows.

12.3a First Offense: Technical foul.

12.3b Second Offense: Technical foul.

12.3c Third Offense: Forfeiture of game.

12.4 Touching or coming into contact with your opponent's rods in any way shall be penalized exactly like jarring, sliding, or lifting.

12.5 **Reset:** If a player has the ball stopped (so his ten-second time limit has started) and set up to shoot, and the ball is moved due to jarring by the opponent, the official present will call "reset" and he will reset the ten-second timer. The player with the ball has the option of setting the ball up again, or ignoring the reset call and playing the ball where it is. The defensive team should not, therefore, relax or look at the official upon hearing the word "reset," but rather should stay on defense.

12.5a A reset call does **not** count as a jarring infraction. However, repeated offenses may be grounds for the official present to call a technical foul on the defensive player causing the reset.

13. Reaching into the Playing Area

13.1 While the ball is in play:

13.1a It is illegal for a player to reach into the play area while the ball is in play without first having permission from the opposing team, whether he touches the ball or not. The penalty for violation of this rule is an automatic technical foul, except during a time-out (*see* 13.1d), or when the player reaching in touches the ball while in play in his own goal area, in which case a point is scored for the opposing team and the ball is re-served just as if it had gone in the goal.

13.1b A spinning ball is considered in play and it is illegal to reach into the playing area to stop a spinning ball, **even if done for an opponent.** The penalty is a technical foul.

13.1c A ball which becomes airborne is still in play until it hits something not a part of the playing area. Do not catch a flying ball over the table.

13.1d During a time-out, the ball is considered to be in play if it was in play at the time that the time-out was called, thereby making it illegal to reach in and/or touch the ball at that time. The penalty is loss of possession if the team reaching in has the ball. Otherwise it is a technical foul.

13.2 It is legal to reach into the playing area at the following times.

13.2a A ball which has gone dead (*see* Dead Ball) is considered out of play and may be touched with the permission of the opposing team.

13.2b A player may wipe shot marks off any part of the table after the ball has been scored or declared dead, and between games. He does **not** need to ask permission of the opposing team.

13.2c Whenever the opposing team grants permission to reach into the playing area, it is legal for the player to do so.

14. Foreign Objects on Field of Play

14.1 If an object should fall on the play field, the team in possession of the ball must stop play so that the object can be removed. There should be nothing on the ends of the table that could fall onto the play field. If the ball strikes an object that has fallen on the play field, it shall be considered out of play, and put back into play as if it has been declared a dead ball.

15. Alterations to the Table

15.1 Playing Area: No changes can be made that would affect the interior playing characteristics of the table by any player. A player cannot wipe sweat or spit or any foreign substance on his hand before wiping ball marks off the table.

15.2 Handles: In regard to the use of substances to improve grip, if a player uses a substance that, upon switching table sides, has left a deposit on the handles, he must immediately clean the handles. If the time necessary to remove the substance exceeds sixty seconds, a technical foul may be called and the player will be prohibited from using the substance again.

16. Distraction

16.1 Any movement or sound made away from the rod where the ball is in play may be judged a distraction. No point made as a result of a distraction will count. Banging the five-man rod or any rod prior to or during a shot is considered a distraction. Also, talking between teammates while the ball is in play may be judged a distraction.

16.2 If a player believes he is being distracted, it is his responsibility to call for an official.

16.3 If a team is judged in violation of this rule and a shot is scored as a result of the distraction, the point will not count and the opposing team will re-serve the ball. If a team is judged in violation of this rule without scoring, the opposing team has the option of continuing play or re-serving the ball.

17. Practice

17.1 Once a match has begun, no player may practice either his serve or his shot on either the table being played on or any other table. This rule applies during time-outs and between games. In order to be considered practice, the following two conditions must both be met: (1) a ball must be on the table; and (2) the player in question must move a ball by making one or more of the playing figures come into contact with the ball.

17.2 Penalty for this infraction is a technical foul, except in the case of 7.7a.

18. Language

18.1 Table talk shall be limited to conversation within a team by players. Comments made directly or indirectly to an opponent, with the exception of honest compliments on play, are not allowed.

18.2 Shouting or calling the attention of the opposing team away from the game shall not be allowed (*see* Distraction). Any shouts or sounds, even of an enthusiastic nature, made while the ball is in play, may be grounds for a technical foul.

18.3 Cursing by a player shall not be allowed and shall carry quick technical fouls. Continued cursing by a player may be cause for forfeiture of games and/or expulsion from the tournament site.

18.4 Cursing by members of the audience shall be cause for expulsion from the tournament site.

18.5 The use of a spotter in the audience shall not be allowed. However, coaching will be allowed during time-outs.

19. Passing

19.1 A pinned or stopped ball on the five-man rod cannot be directly advanced to the three-man rod of the same team. It must touch at least two playing figures as it is put into the motion of a pass.

    19.1a A stopped ball is defined as a ball whose motion has stopped for a full second within reach of one of the playing figures of a five-man rod. A ball does not, however, have to be pinned, either to the wall or the play field, for a full second—this rule applies as soon as the ball is pinned.

    19.1b The pinned rule is hard to enforce and may require the judgment of an official. The ruling will be based on whether the ball was caused to stop or change direction or speed due to a pin directly prior to being advanced.

    19.1c A pinned or stopped ball may be shot on goal. To be considered a shot, the ball must either go into the goal, be blocked by the opposing goalie's men, or hit the back wall. If the attempted shot is blocked by the opposing five-man rod and then caught by the shooter's three-man, it shall be declared an illegal pass.

19.2 Before attempting a pass from the five-man rod, the player cannot make the ball strike either side wall or side strip of the table more than twice. It makes no difference which wall the ball touches—a total of two times is all that is allowed. If the ball goes to the wall a third time, it must be advanced in the motion of a pass or shot.

    19.2a Defensive Trap: If an opponent's pass or shot is stopped by trapping it against the side wall, that does not count as one of the two times allowed to touch the wall by the player who made the trap and is now in possession of the ball on his five-man rod.

19.3 Passing from the Two- and One-Man Rods: Rules 19.1, 19.1a, and 19.1b also apply to a pass from the two- or one-man rod to the same team's five-man rod. However, once a ball is forwarded from either the two- or one-man rods, if it should strike an opposing team's playing figures, that ball is no longer considered a pass but a live ball that may be legally caught by any player.

19.4 **Penalty for an Illegal Pass:** If a team violates the above rules of passing, the opposing team re-serves the ball.

20. Time of Possession

20.1 Enforcement of the time of possession rule shall be made only by an authorized tournament official.

20.2 Possession of the ball at any one rod shall be limited to twenty seconds, except the five-man rod, which has a ten-second limit, by the end of which time period the player in possession must advance the ball to or past at least one rod of the opposing team.

20.3 Once a ball is stopped or pinned on any rod except the five-man rod (*see* 20.4), the player has ten seconds to shoot or pass the ball. Should the player move the ball to another figure, the ten-second limit will stop, and then start over again if the ball is again stopped or pinned, provided the player does not exceed the twenty-second total rod time limit, which is continuous, regardless of the movement of the ball. If the ball is released from the pin position, the ten-second clock is reset. Dribbling the ball does not constitute release from the pin.

20.4 On the five-man rod, once the ball is stopped or pinned, the player has three seconds to shoot or pass the ball.

20.5 A spinning ball that is within reach of a playing figure shall be considered to be in that rod's possession and all time limits shall continue. Players must make an honest effort to gain possession of a spinning ball that is within reach; however, if the spinning ball is not within reach, the time limits are not in effect.

20.6 **PENALTY:** Penalty for three-man delay is loss of possession to opposing goalie. The goalie shall put the ball back into play as if it had been declared a dead ball. Penalty for delay at any other rod is loss of possession to the opposing forward for serve.

21. Match Time Limit

21.1 Best of five matches shall be limited to one hour of play from the time the match is first called. Best of three matches shall be limited to thirty-five minutes from the time the match is first called.

21.2 If the specified time limit expires before the match has been completed, an official will announce to the players that a ten-minute overtime period will begin at that time. If the overtime period ends before the match has been completed, the winner of the match shall be the player or team which has won the most games, or, if the teams have won an equal number of games, it shall be the team that has scored the most points in the game in progress, **after** the ball in play at the time that the overtime period expires has been scored. If the teams have won an equal number of games and scored an equal number of points after this ball has been scored, one more ball shall be played to determine the winner of the match.

21.3 Time-outs called within the regular time limit of a match shall be counted against the total amount of time left to play. However, time-outs do **not** count against the ten minutes in the overtime period (a time-out then would stop the clock).

21.4 Should an official judge that a team has caused an **illegal delay** during an overtime period, he may call a technical foul on that team and add one minute of play to the overtime period for each infraction.

22. Forfeiture

22.1 Once a match has been called, both teams should report immediately to the designated table. If you are at the table and your opponent has not yet arrived, you should wait three minutes only before going to the stage and filling out a card for the first recall. Return to the table, wait another three minutes, and if the opposing team does not arrive, return to the stage and fill out a card for the second recall. Wait three more minutes before the third recall. After three recalls, a team has one more minute before forfeiture of the first game. The above procedure is repeated until either the team appears at the table or the entire match is forfeited. This gives a team a total of ten minutes before forfeiture of a game. Enforcement of this rule shall be the responsibility of the tournament director.

23. Technical Foul

23.1 If, in the judgment of an authorized tournament official, either team competing in a match is at any time in flagrant or intentional violation of these rules of play, a technical foul may be called on the offending team.

23.2 When a technical foul is called, play shall stop and the ball awarded to the opponents of the offending team at its three-man rod. One shot will be taken (players must remain at the same positions during the technical foul shot as they were prior to the call), after which play shall stop. If it scores or not, the ball shall be put back into play at the spot it was in when the technical was called. If the ball was in motion, it will be put back into play as if it had been declared dead in that spot.

23.3 Further violations of a flagrant or intentional nature shall carry additional technical fouls. The official may announce at any time after the first technical foul is called on a team that further violation by that team shall be cause for forfeiture of the match.

24. Rules Decisions and Appeals

24.1 Any player may request an official at any time during a game (*see* "Official" Time-Out, 7.10).

24.2 If the controversy involves an interpretation of the rules and the official was not present at the time the events in question transpired, the official shall make the most equitable decision possible under the circumstances. Decisions of this nature may be appealed, but it must be done immediately in the manner prescribed in 24.3.

24.3 **APPEALS:** In order to appeal a decision, a player must file that appeal with the tournament director before the ball being played at the time of the controversy is put back into play. An appeal concerning the forfeiture of a match must be filed before the team that won by forfeiture has begun its next match.

24.4 All appeals shall be considered by the tournament director and at least one member of the WTSA Board. All decisions on appeals are final.

24.5 If a controversy involves a question of judgment, and the official is present at the time the events in question transpired, his decision is final and no appeal may be made.

25. Code of Ethics

25.1 Any action of an unsportsmanlike or unethical nature during tournament play, in the tournament room, or in or on the grounds of the host facility will be considered a violation of the code of ethics.

25.2 **Penalty:** The penalty for breaking the code of ethics may be forfeiture of a game or match, expulsion from the tournament, and/or a fine not to exceed $500. Whether or not the code of ethics has been broken, and the appropriate penalty for the infraction will be determined by the tournament director and at least one member of the WTSA Board.

26. Tournament Director

26.1 The administration of tournament play shall be the responsibility of the tournament director, appointed by the tournament sponsor and approved by the WTSA.

Appendix II:
Money Winners, Championships, and Awards

1975—TOP TWENTY MONEY WINNERS

1. Dan Kaiser	$14,160.00	11. Eddy Whitesides	$5,520.00
2. Ken Rivera	11,145.00	12. Brent Bednar	5,500.00
3. Johnny Lott	8,362.50	13. Paul Daltas	5,402.50
4. Mike Bowers	7,287.50	14. Ed Tuhkanen	5,012.50
5. Karin von Otterstedt	7,057.50	15. Bill Sumption	4,725.00
6. Steve Simon	6,137.50	16. Lori Schranz	4,717.50
7. Lane Hunnicutt	5,797.50	17. Guy Volgelbacher	4,182.50
8. Tom Hansen	5,697.50	18. Vicki Chalgren	4,090.00
9. Gary Pfeil	5,645.00	19. Faye McWilliams	4,032.50
10. Mike Belz	5,587.50	20. Mark Strand	3,836.25

1976—TOP TWENTY MONEY WINNERS

1. Mike Belz	$18,250.00	11. Lori Schranz	$8,212.50
2. Brent Bednar	18,200.00	12. Bev Froom	7,282.50
3. Steve Simon	15,375.00	13. Karin Gililland	6,805.00
4. Johnny Lott	12,850.00	14. Tim Burns	6,650.00
5. Dan Kaiser	12,787.50	15. Vicki Chalgren	6,600.00
6. Mike Bowers	12,775.00	16. Mark Scheuer	6,262.50

7. Jim Zellick	11,750.00	17. Jim Wiswell	5,900.00
8. Marcio Bonilla	11,075.00	18. Gary Pfeil	5,837.50
9. Rick Beberg	10,550.50	19. John Shotwell	5,412.50
10. Guy Volgelbacher	8,262.50	20. Dan Kocak	5,362.50

1977—TOP TWENTY MONEY WINNERS

1. Doug Furry	$25,190.00	11. Ken Alwell	$5,675.00
2. Steve Simon	13,475.00	12. Steve Malean	4,825.00
3. Todd Loffredo	13,000.00	13. Mike Belz	4,700.00
4. Gil Jackson	12,750.00	14. Jerry Knowles	4,612.50
5. Jim Wiswell	9,450.00	15. Paul Reynolds	4,500.00
6. Rick Martin	8,475.00	16. Mark Crowell	4,450.00
7. Johnny Lott	7,825.00	17. Karin Gililland	4,350.00
8. Mike Bowers	6,925.00	18. Lori Schranz	4,162.50
9. Mark Scheuer	6,800.00	19. Gayle Harding	3,935.00
10. Tim Burns	6,100.00	20. Faye McWilliams	3,812.50

1978-1979—TOP TWENTY MONEY WINNERS

1. Jim Wiswell	$40,560.00	11. Mike Bowers	$11,980.00
2. Doug Furry	39,635.00	12. Carrie Crowell	11,785.00
3. Dan Kaiser	38,365.00	13. Brent Bednar	10,935.00
4. Tom Spear	33,005.00	14. Ken Rivera	9,895.00
5. Lori Schranz	23,230.00	15. Mark Crowell	9,650.00
6. Paul Reynolds	18,090.00	16. Gil Jackson	9,395.00
7. Todd Loffredo	16,750.00	17. Tim Burns	9,125.00
8. Rick Martin	15,320.00	18. Mike Belz	8,615.00
9. Ken Alwell	14,575.00	19. Craig Legens	8,355.00
10. Shawn Coonrod	12,110.00	20. Duane Pratt	7,900.00

TOP TEN ALL-TIME CAREER MONEY WINNERS

(Earnings compiled in competition on the professional tour from 1975 through 1980. Winnings include only official WTSA tournament winnings.)

1. Doug Furry	$85,002.50	6. Tom Spear	$46,220.00
2. Dan Kaiser	77,502.50	7. Johnny Lott	45,822.50
3. Jim Wiswell	69,210.00	8. Brent Bednar	43,897.50
4. Mike Bowers	53,367.50	9. Steve Simon	42,462.50
5. Lori Schranz	49,602.50	10. Mike Belz	39,352.50

WORLD CHAMPIONSHIP FINALISTS—1975

Open Doubles

1. Dan Kaiser
   Ken Rivera
2. Brent Bednar
   Mike Belz
3. Johnny Lott
   Paul Daltas

Singles

1. Steve Simon
2. Doug Furry
3. Lane Hunnicutt

Women's Doubles

1. Karin Gililland
   Lori Schranz
2. Faye McWilliams
   Gayle Harding
3. Vicki Chalgren
   Karen Harada

Mixed Doubles

1. Karin Gililland
   Bill Sumption
2. Johnny Lott
   Vicki Chalgren
3. Gayle Harding
   Dan Kaiser

WORLD CHAMPIONSHIP FINALISTS—1976

Open Doubles

1. Brent Bednar
   Mike Belz
2. Jim Zellick
   Marcio Bonilla
3. Dan Kocak
   John Shotwell

Singles

1. Dan Kaiser
2. Steve Simon
3. Johnny Lott

Mixed Doubles

1. Bev Froom
   Rick Beberg
2. Johnny Lott
   Vicki Chalgren
3. Gary Pfeil
   Lori Schranz

Women's Doubles

1. Karin Gililland
   Lori Schranz
2. Kit Lewis
   Jeanne Thyberg
3. Marla Gibson
   Joyce Treblehorn

WORLD CHAMPIONSHIP FINALISTS—1977

Open Doubles
1. Todd Loffredo
   Gil Jackson
2. Ken Alwell
   Mark Scheuer
3. Jim Wiswell
   Doug Furry

Singles
1. Rick Martin
2. Paul Reynolds
3. Steve Malean

Mixed Doubles
1. Steve Simon
   Gayle Harding
2. Faye McWilliams
   Jim Wiswell
3. Bob Curtin
   Georgia Schabilion

Women's Doubles
1. Karin Gililland
   Lori Schranz
2. Kit Lewis
   Jan Alexander
3. Carrie Westbrook
   Bev Froom

WORLD CHAMPIONSHIP FINALISTS—1978-1979

Open Doubles
1. Jim Wiswell
   Doug Furry
2. Dan Kaiser
   Tom Spear
3. Paul Reynolds
   Ken Rivera

Singles
1. Dan Kaiser
2. Tom Spear
3. Johnny Horton

Mixed Doubles
1. Tom Spear
   Carrie Crowell
2. Todd Loffredo
   Sharon Doane
3. Ken Alwell
   Bev Froom

Women's Doubles
1. Carrie Crowell
   Lori Schranz
2. Jan Alexander
   Sharon Doane
3. Marianne Kohler
   Becky Spillman

WORLD CHAMPIONSHIP FINALISTS—1980

Open Doubles

1. Tim Burns
   Mike Bowers
2. Dan Kaiser
   Rick Martin

Singles

1. Johnny Lott
2. Alwood Makekau

Mixed Doubles

1. Jim Wiswell
   Lori Schranz
2. Gregg Perrie
   Bev Froom

Women's Doubles

1. Carrie Crowell
   Lori Schranz
2. Rochelle Creegan
   Shima Washburn

AWARDS

Player of the Year

1976	Rick Beberg
1977	Mike Bowers
1978	Dan Kaiser
1979	Tom Spear

Professionalism Awards

1975	Karin Gililland, Gary Pfeil
1976	Vicki Chalgren, Mike Bowers
1977	Lori Schranz, Doug Furry
1978	Lori Schranz, Tom Spear
1979	Bev Froom, Mike Bowers

Sportsmanship Award

1975	Faye McWilliams, Bill Sumption
1976	Faye McWilliams, Mark Scheuer
1977	Debbie Wilson, Mike Belz
1978	Becky Spillman, Rick Martin
1979	Bev Froom, Gregg Perrie

Best-Dressed Award

1978 Pro—Jim Wiswell, Doug Furry
     Novice—Tony Cinca, Brad Pizo
1979 Pro—Maggie Tolizano, Bonnie Slonaker
     Novice—All Arapahoe Sports Center Teams

LIST OF HONORS: ETU EUROPEAN CHAMPIONSHIPS

Doubles

1977 Diakonis-Karkalakis, Belgium
1978 Pascal Gressier-Bernardo Borrelli, Belgium
1979 Lucas Skara-Rigo Skara, Germany

Singles

1978 Michel Burgener, Switzerland
1979 Pascal Gressier, Belgium

Goalie War

1978 M. Hanseer, Belgium
1979 G. Ferrari, Belgium

National Teams

Year	1st	2nd	3rd	4th
1976	1. Holland	2. Belgium	3. Germany	
1977	1. Belgium	2. Holland	3. Switzerland	4. Germany
1978	1. Belgium	2. Switzerland	3. Holland	4. Germany
1979	1. Belgium	2. Luxembourg	3. Holland	

Club Teams

1977 Smidter Boys, Holland
1978 Millen TVV, Belgium
1979 Millen TVV, Belgium

Cup Championship

1978 Herstal KC, Belgium
1979 Stardust Mecheven, Belgium

Belgian Doubles Championship

1975	Strasser-Collignon, Ans
1976	Stevens-Hanseer, Millen
1977	Strasser-Collignon, Ans
1978	Pirlet-Hanseer, Millen
1979	Kohnen-Hustings, Liege

Swiss Doubles Championship

1975	Herbert Perrin-Yvon Perrin
1976	Michel Demonsant-Eric Gaillard
1977	Michel Demonsant, Eric Gaillard
1978	Herbert Perrin-Anselme Perrin

Swiss Singles Championship

1975	Herbert Perrin
1976	Herbert Perrin
1977	Michel Burgener
1978	Michel Burgener

Belgian Singles Championship

1975	John Melahrinidis
1976	Pascal Gressier
1977	Pascal Gressier
1978	Pascal Gressier
1979	John Paul Pirlet

Belgian Club Teams Championship

1974-1975	Millen TVV
1975-1976	La Paix Etterbeek
1976-1977	La Paix Etterbeek
1977-1978	Millen TVV
1978-1979	Millen TVV

Appendix III: Professional Player Biographies

THE PIONEERS

Rick Beberg

Rick Beberg was the first player from the West Coast to strike it big on the professional tour. In 1976, Beberg (then a novice) quit his job in Chico, California, and set out on a journey that would establish him as one of the top players on the tour and earn him the 1976 World Mixed Doubles title, in addition to

Rick Beberg

Marcio Bonilla

Karin Gililland

being voted the 1976 player of the year. Beberg has since retired, but his influence on foosball remains evident from the many top players coming out of California.

Marcio Bonilla

No player has accomplished more for the sport of foosball than Marcio Bonilla. Originally from Costa Rica, Bonilla now resides in Seattle, Washington, and is one of the old-time greats of foosball, having played for more than twenty-five years. A two-time world champion and a businessman/promoter of the game, Bonilla has traveled extensively throughout the United States, Canada, Argentina, and Europe, working with players and establishments to increase awareness of the sport of foosball.

Karin Gililland (formerly Karin von Otterstedt)

One of the first competitive women in the history of foosball, Karin Gililland is ranked among the greatest players ever to have played the game. Teamed with Lori Schranz, Gililland won the 1975, 1976, and 1977 World Women's Doubles titles, not to mention the 1975 World Mixed title and a fourth-place finish in open doubles at the 1976 World Championship (the best finish ever by a woman in open doubles).

Gary Pfeil   Tom Hansen (left) Billy Sumption (right)

Gary Pfeil

Hailing from Dallas, Texas, Pfeil was best known for his precision style of play and a devastating pull shot, which earned him the 1974 World Mixed Doubles title plus numerous tour championships. Pfeil's professional appearance, attitude, and good sportsmanship influenced many upcoming rookies and professional players to better represent the sport of foosball.

Billy Sumption and Tom Hansen

The first professionals to come out of the state of Minnesota, Hansen and Sumption teamed up to finish as runners-up in the 1974 World Championship. Sumption went on to claim the 1975 World Mixed Doubles title, and Hansen later teamed up with Ed Tuhkanen to win several major doubles titles.

Aside from their numerous achievements as players, Hansen and Sumption introduced thousands of players throughout the Midwest to the sport of foosball. Top professionals such as Wiswell, Furry, Alwell, Belz, and Bednar, to name a few, will all tell you how much Hansen and Sumption have been a factor in the development of their games.

Ken Alwell   Brent Bednar

THE STARS

Ken Alwell

Hometown: Roseville, Minnesota
First tour victory: 1977 $10,000 Open—Champaign, Illinois—doubles
Regular position: Forward
Favorite shot: Pushkick
Usual partner: Varies
Accomplishments: 1977 World Doubles runner-up, 1979 $100,000 Chicago Super Doubles—runner-up—plus tour victories in singles, doubles, and mixed doubles.

Brent Bednar

Hometown: Cedar, Minnesota
First tour victory: $10,000 Seattle Open—January, 1976—doubles
Regular position: Goalie
Favorite shot: Pull shot
Usual partner: Mike Belz
Accomplishments: 1975 World Doubles runner-up, 1976 World Doubles champion, 1978 Super Doubles runner-up, plus major tour victories in doubles and mixed doubles.

APPENDIX III 163

Mike Belz   Mike Bowers

Mike Belz

Hometown: New Brighton, Minnesota
First tour victory: $25,000 St. Louis Open—March, 1976—doubles
Regular position: Forward
Favorite shot: Pushkick
Usual partner: Brent Bednar
Accomplishments: 1975 World Doubles runner-up, 1976 World Doubles champion, third place in 1976 World Mixed Doubles, plus major tour victories in doubles and mixed doubles.

Mike Bowers

Hometown: Littleton, Colorado
First tour victory: $10,000 Atlanta Open—March, 1975—singles
Regular position: Goalie
Favorite shot: Pull shot
Usual partner: Tim Burns
Accomplishments: 1973 and 1974 World Singles champion, 1980 World Doubles champion, major tour victories in singles, doubles, and mixed doubles, plus being voted the 1977 player of the year.

Michel Burgener   Tim Burns

Michel Burgener

Hometown: Geneva, Switzerland
First tour victory: 1979 $100,000 Chicago Open—first-place singles—November, 1979
Regular position: Forward
Favorite shot: Frontpin series
Usual partner: Perret Philippe
Accomplishments: Four-time Swiss National Doubles champion, ten-time Swiss National Singles champion, dating back to 1964, plus the 1978 European Singles title and first in singles at the 1979 Chicago $100,000 Open.

Tim "Zeek" Burns

Hometown: Aurora, Colorado
First tour victory: 1976 Portland Open—doubles
Regular position: Forward
Favorite shot: Pull shot
Usual partner: Mike Bowers
Accomplishments: Two-time Portland Open Doubles champion, 1977 $100,000 Minneapolis Open—singles—plus 1980 World Doubles champion.

Doug Furry

Bob Gibson

Doug Furry

Hometown: Hoyt Lakes, Minnesota
First tour victory: $25,000 St. Louis Open—August, 1976—singles
Regular position: Goalie
Favorite shot: Pull shot
Usual partner: Jim Wiswell
Accomplishments: 1977 Super Singles champion, 1978 Super Doubles champion, 1979 World Open Doubles champion, plus numerous tour victories. Doug Furry is currently the all-time leading career money winner, with more than $85,000 in earnings.

Bob Gibson

Hometown: Westminster, Colorado
First tour victory: $50,000 Cleveland Open—September, 1979—pro singles
Regular position: Forward
Favorite shot: Pull shot
Usual partner: Gil Jackson
Accomplishments: First-place singles—1979 $50,000 Cleveland Open—1979 $50,000 Syracuse Open—first-place doubles.

 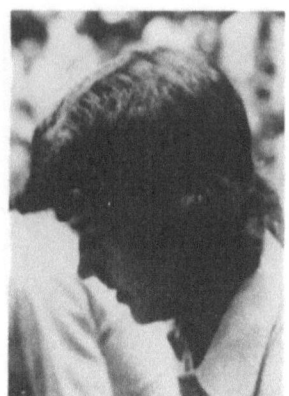

Pascal Gressier · Gil Jackson

Pascal Gressier

Hometown: Brussels, Belgium
First tour victory: 1978 $100,000 Chicago Open—first-place pro-am
Regular position: Forward
Favorite shot: Frontpin series
Usual partner: Bernardo Borrelli
Accomplishments: Three-time Belgium National Singles champion, plus 1978 European Doubles title and 1979 European Singles title.

Gil Jackson

Hometown: Aurora, Colorado
First tour victory: 1977 World Doubles champion—November, 1977
Regular position: Goalie
Favorite shot: Pull shot
Usual partner: Bob Gibson
Accomplishments: 1977 World Doubles champion, 1979 $50,000 Cleveland Open—first-place singles—1979 $50,000 Syracuse Open—first-place doubles—plus numerous first-place finishes in goalie war.

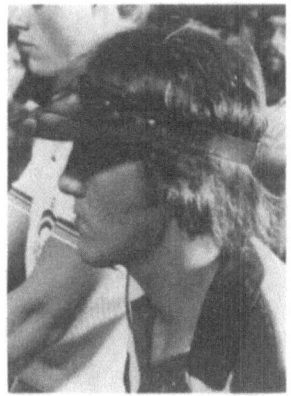 

Dan Kaiser   Todd Loffredo

Dan Kaiser

Hometown: Portland, Oregon
First tour victory: $2,000 Salt Lake Open—January, 1975—doubles
Regular position: Goalie
Favorite shot: Pull shot
Usual partner: Varies
Accomplishments: 1975 World Doubles champion, 1976 World Singles champion, 1978 World Singles champion, plus being voted 1978 player of the year.

Todd Loffredo

Hometown: Littleton, Colorado
First tour victory: 1977 World Doubles champion—November, 1977
Regular position: Forward
Favorite shot: Pull shot
Usual partner: Varies
Accomplishments: 1977 World Doubles champion, 1979 World Mixed Doubles runner-up, 1979 St. Louis Master Invitational—first place—plus tour victories in every event, including goalie war.

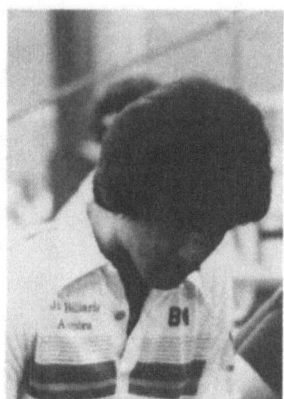

Alwood Makekau   Ben Rivera

Alwood Makekau

Hometown: Tacoma, Washington
First tour victory: Vancouver $10,000—first-place doubles—January, 1979
Regular position: Forward
Favorite shot: Pull shot
Usual partner: Dave McWeeny
Accomplishments: Several first-place tour victories in open doubles, and runner-up in World Singles—1980.

Ben Rivera

Hometown: Los Angeles, California
First tour victory: $100,000 Super Doubles—November, 1979
Regular position: Forward
Favorite shot: Pull shot
Usual partner: Varies
Accomplishments: First-place tour victories in doubles and mixed doubles, including a $20,000 first-place finish in Super Doubles II.

Lori Schranz

Steve Simon

Lori Schranz

Hometown: Dallas, Texas
First tour victory: $50,000 Denver Mixed Doubles—May, 1974
Regular position: Goalie
Favorite shot: Pull shot
Usual partner: Carrie Crowell and Jim Wiswell
Accomplishments: 1975, 1976, 1977, 1979 World Women's Doubles champion, 1974 and 1980 World Mixed Doubles champion, women's all-time leading career money winner, plus being voted most professional player in both 1977 and 1978.

Steve Simon

Hometown: San Antonio, Texas
First tour victory: 1975 World Singles champion—September, 1975
Regular position: Forward
Favorite shot: Pushkick
Usual partner: Johnny Lott
Accomplishments: 1975 World Singles champion, 1976 World Singles runner-up, 1977 World Mixed Doubles champion, plus numerous tour victories, including a string of eleven

Tom Spear   Jim Wiswell

tournaments in a row in which Steve made it to the finals in singles, out of which he won eight first places.

Tom Spear

Hometown: Aurora, Colorado
First tour victory: $10,000 Denver Open—April, 1978—doubles
Regular position: Forward
Favorite shot: Pull shot
Usual partner: Varies
Accomplishments: 1978 Chicago $100,000 Open—first-place doubles—1979 World Singles runner-up, 1979 World Mixed Doubles champion, 1979 World Doubles runner-up, plus being voted the 1978 most professional player.

Jim Wiswell

Hometown: Hoyt Lakes, Minnesota
First tour victory: $10,000 Rock Island Open—May, 1976—singles
Regular position: Forward
Favorite shot: Pull shot
Usual partner: Doug Furry
Accomplishments: 1978 Super Doubles champion, 1979 World Open Doubles champion, 1980 World Mixed champion, plus major tour victories in singles, doubles, and mixed doubles.

Index

A

Alterations to the table, rules governing, 145
Alwell, Ken, 162, *illus.* 13, 162
Angle-down pass, 49, *illus.* 50
Angle-up pass, 49, *illus.* 50
Associated College Unions-International (ACU-I), 118-119
Awards, 156-157

B

Backpin series shot, 67-68, *illus.* 67
Bail, meaning of, 27
Bait, meaning of, 27
Ball in play, rules governing, 137
Ball out of play, rule governing, 137
Ball release, 42-44, *illus.* 43
Bank shots, 70, 100-102, *illus.* 101
Basic shooting techniques and options, 53-74
Bearings, maintenance of, 25
Beberg, Rick, 12, 159-160, *illus.* 159
Bednar, Brent, 11-12, 18, 162, *illus.* 162
Belz, Mike, 11-12, 18, 163, *illus.* 163
Between, meaning of, 27
Blattspieler, Steve, 10
Bonilla, Marcio, 7, 11, 160, *illus.* 160

172 INDEX

Bowers, Mike, 7-12, 19-20, 163, *illus.* 20, 163
Briggs, Jack, 7-8
Burgener, Michel, 164, *illus.* 164
Burns, Tim, 19-20, 164, *illus.* 20, 164

C

Camp, meaning of, 28
Cannonball grip, 37, *illus.* 38
Catching the ball, 51-52
Chalgren, Vicki, 8
Change of positions, rule governing, 141-142
Code of ethics, rules governing, 151
College tournaments, 118-119, *illus.* 119
Common rules and etiquette, 112-116
Conditioning and preparation for tournament play, 94-96
Coonrod, Shawn, 14
Crossover defense, goalie position, 80, *illus.* 81
Crowell, Carrie, 18, 20
Cup drop serve, 32, *illus.* 32

D

Daltas, Paul, 10
Dead ball, rules governing, 137-138
Deadman, meaning of, 28
Distraction, rules governing, 145
Double, meaning of, 28
Draw your partner (DYP), meaning of, 28
Drill, meaning of, 28
Drop, meaning of, 28

E

European Table Soccer Union (ETU), 3

F

Fallon, Dale, 8
Far, meaning of, 28
Fast wall pass, 47, *illus.* 48
Finger grip, 38, *illus.* 39
Finger serve, 33, *illus.* 33-34
Five-man defense, forward position, 86-87
Five-man passing, pro tip on, 49-51
Five-man passing, variations on, 51
Flat-footed stance, 35, *illus.* 36
Folk, Larry, 7
Foos Noos, 8, 134
Foosball accessories, 25-26
Foosball clothing, 26
Foosball gloves, 25-26, *illus.* 26
Foosball table assembly, 23
Foosball table maintenance, 23-25
Foosball table selection, 23
Foreign objects on the field of play, rule governing, 144-145
Forfeiture, rule governing, 149-150
Fork defense, forward position, 87-88, *illus.* 88
Forward position defensive techniques, 86-89, *illus.* 88-89
Forward position offensive techniques, 46-52
Forward position tips, 92-94

Four-on-four (or four-man) game, 106-108, *illus.* 107
Frontpin series shot, 68-69, *illus.* 68
Froom, Bev, 12, 20
Furry, Doug, 11-14, 18-19, 165, *illus.* 15, 165

G

Game point. *See* Meatball
Game variations, 106-111
Get down, meaning of, 28
Gibson, Bob, 165, *illus.* 165
Gibson, Marla, 8
Gililland, John, 8
Gililland, Karin, 12-14, 160, *illus.* 131, 160. *See also* von Otterstedt, Karin
Goalie booties, 26
Goalie defense development, 85-86
Goalie defensive techniques, 80-86, *illus.* 79, 81, 84
Goalie defensive tips, 83, 91-92
Goalie field goal attempt, 105, *illus.* 104
Goalie offensive development, 76-77
Goalie offensive techniques, 70-76, *illus.* 75-76
Goalie offensive tips, 73, 90-91
Goalie pass, 76, *illus.* 76
Goalie stance, 37
Goalie war, 109-111, *illus.* 110
Gressier, Pascal, 166, *illus.* 166
Grip, 37-42
Grip cream, 26
Grip products, 25-26
Gut, meaning of, 28

H

Hansen, Tom, 7-10, 161, *illus.* 161
Harding, Gayle, 10, 14
Hole, meaning of, 28
Hunnicutt, Lane, 10

I

In-and-out, meaning of, 28
Inside, meaning of, 28

J

Jackson, Gil, 14, 166, *illus.* 13, 166
Jarring, rules governing, 142-143

K

Kaiser, Dan, 10-12, 18-19, 167, *illus.* 15, 167
Kibitzing, meaning of, 28
Kicker tables, 2
Kyle, Edie, 10

L

Language, rules governing, 146
Le Soir Illustre, 1
Leg back stance, 35, *illus.* 36
List of honors, ETU European Championships, 157-158
Local tournaments, 118
Loffredo, Todd, 14, 18, 167, *illus.* 13, 167
Long, meaning of, 28
Lott, Johnny, 11, 19, *illus.* 20
Louisiana shuffle defense, 83-84, *illus.* 84

M

McWilliams, Faye, 10
Makekau, Alwood, 168, *illus.* 168
Martin, Rick, 14
Match starting, rules governing, 135
Match time limit, rules governing, 149
Meatball, meaning of, 29
Mental aspect of foosball, pro tip on, 98–99
Middle, meaning of, 29

N

Near, meaning of, 29
Nit, meaning of, 29

O

Offense development, 68
Option, meaning of, 29
Outside, meaning of, 29
Overall ball control, 44

P

Palm roll grip, 38–42, *illus.* 41
Passing for five-man offense, pro tip on, 93–94
Passing from the five-man to the three-man, 46–52
Passing, rules governing, 146–148
Peppard, Lee, 5–9, 20, *illus.* 6
Perrin, Herbert, 10, *illus.* 20
Perrin, Yvon, 10, *illus.* 20
Pfeil, Gary, 7–10, 161, *illus.* 161
Pick. *See* Stuff

Pin bank offense, goalie position, 72–73
Pits, meaning of, 29
Point scored on an in-and-out, rules governing, 141
Pop-out. *See* In-and-out
Practice, rules governing, 146
Professional instruction at tournaments, 123–124
Professional tournaments, 119–120, *illus.* 120
Pull pass, 75, *illus.* 75
Pull shot, pro tip on, 60
Pull shot for women, pro tip on, 131–132
Pull shot offense, 58–62, *illus.* 59, 61
Pull shot options, 60–62, *illus.* 61, 63
Pullkick offense, 62–64, *illus.* 63
Pullkick options, 64–65, *illus.* 65
Purcell, Joe, 8
Push shot offense, 66–67, *illus.* 66
Push shot options, 66–67, *illus.* 66
Pushkick, pro tip on, 57
Pushkick offense, 53–55, *illus.* 54
Pushkick options, 55–58, *illus.* 56

R

Race defense, goalie position, 82–83
Random defense, goalie position, 84–85
Ranking of professional players, 120–122

Razzle dazzle, meaning of, 29
Reaching into the playing area, rules governing, 143–144
Rebound smash shot, 102, *illus.* 101
Reject. *See* Stuff
Rivera, Ken, 10–11, 168, *illus.* 110, 168
Rod lubricant, 25
Rogers, Cal, 8–10, 20, *illus.* 9
Rosengart, Lucien, 1–2
Rosin, 26
Rules decisions and appeals, rules governing, 150–151

S

Saturday Night Foosball. *See* Razzle dazzle
Scheuer, Mark, 12, *illus.* 13
Schranz, Lori, 8–14, 18–20, 130–132, 169, *illus.* 131, 169
Serve, 31–34
Serve, rules governing, 135–136
Set bank shot, 70–72, *illus.* 71
Set position, meaning of, 29
Shooting from the three-man, 52–68
Simon, Steve, 10–14, 169, *illus.* 169
Skunk, meaning of, 29
Snider, Joe, 7
Solid rod, advantages of, 6
Somekawa, Gordy, 8
Spear, Tom, 14, 18, 170, *illus.* 15, 170
Spike. *See* Stuff
Spinning, rules governing, 142
Split. *See* Between and Middle
Split for middle pull shot, 60, *illus.* 61

Squib. *See* Stub
Stance, 35–37
Standard defense, goalie position, 80, *illus.* 79
Stick pass, 47, *illus.* 48
Straight-in pull shot, 60–62, *illus.* 61
Stub, meaning of, 29
Stuff, meaning of, 29–30
Subsequent serves, rules governing, 136–137
Sumption, Billy, 7–11, 161, *illus.* 161
Sweatball. *See* Meatball

T

Table components, *illus.* 24, 46
Table cover, 26
Table sides, rule governing, 141
Technical foul, rules governing, 150
Telegraph, meaning of, 30
Three-on-three (or three-man) game, 107
Three-man-to-five-man reverse smash shot, 102, *illus.* 103
Time of possession, rules governing, 148
Time-out, rules governing, 138–141
Top Ten All-Time Career Money Winners, 153
Top Twenty Money Winners, 1975–1979, 152–153
Tournament director, rule governing, 151
Tournament events, 122–123, *illus.* 123
Tournament procedures, 124–129

Tournament Soccer (Company), 5
Tournament Soccer table, 22, *illus.* 22
Tournament Soccer's First Five Years (chart), 16–17
Trick shots, 100–105
Triple, meaning of, 30
Tuhkanen, Ed, 10
Turnover, meaning of, 30
Two-on-one game, 111
Two-ball rollerball, 108–109
Two-man-to-one-man reverse smash shot, 105

V

Visors, 26
Vogelbacher, Guy, 10
von Otterstedt, Karin, 8–11. *See also* Gililland, Karin

W

Wachlte, Karen, 8
Whiff, meaning of, 30
Whitesides, Ed, 7, 10
Wiswell, Jim, 14, 18, 20, 170, *illus.* 15, 170
World Championship Finalists, 1975–1980, 154–156
World Table Soccer Association (WTSA), 8, 134
World Table Soccer Association Rules of Play, 135–151
Wrist shots, 73–74

Z

Zellick, Jim, 12
Zone defense, forward position, 88–89, *illus.* 89

www.ingramcontent.com/pod-product-compliance
Lightning Source LLC
Chambersburg PA
CBHW030112010526
44116CB00005B/219